First World War
and Army of Occupation
War Diary
France, Belgium and Germany

35 DIVISION
Headquarters, Branches and Services
Royal Army Ordnance Corps
Deputy Assistant Director Ordnance Services
2 March 1916 - 31 March 1919

WO95/2473/2

The Naval & Military Press Ltd
www.nmarchive.com
Published in association with The National Archives

Published by

The Naval & Military Press Ltd

Unit 10 Ridgewood Industrial Park,

Uckfield, East Sussex,

TN22 5QE England

Tel: +44 (0) 1825 749494

www.naval-military-press.com

www.nmarchive.com

This diary has been reprinted in facsimile from the original. Any imperfections are inevitably reproduced and the quality may fall short of modern type and cartographic standards.

© **Crown Copyright**
Images reproduced by permission of The National Archives, London, England, 2015.

Contents

Document type	Place/Title	Date From	Date To
Heading	WO95/2473/2 35 Div Mar'16-Apr; 19 Dep. Ass. Director Ordnance Service.		
Heading	35th Division Divl Troops. D.A.D. Ordnance Services Mar 1916-Apr 1919		
Heading	War Diary D.A.D.O.S. 35th Division March 1916. Vol 16		
War Diary		02/03/1916	30/04/1916
War Diary	In The Field	04/05/1916	30/09/1917
Heading	War Diary D.A.D. Ordce 35 Divn. Period-Feby 1-28th 1918. Volume No. 2		
War Diary	In The Field	01/10/1917	31/10/1917
Miscellaneous	Statement showing principal terms of work performed in war Shops during the month of October.		
War Diary	In the field	01/11/1917	30/11/1917
Miscellaneous	Summary of principal terms of work performed in Divl. Shops Nov.	10/10/1917	10/10/1917
War Diary	In the field	01/12/1917	01/12/1917
War Diary	Peselhoek	01/12/1917	09/12/1917
War Diary	Proven	11/12/1917	15/12/1917
War Diary	In the field	17/12/1917	29/12/1917
Heading	War Diary. D.A.D.O.S. 35th Divn. Period-1st to. 31st January. 1918. Volume No. 2		
War Diary	In the field	02/01/1918	31/01/1918
War Diary	Statement showing principal terms of work performed in Divl. Shops during January 1918	02/01/1918	31/01/1918
War Diary	In the field	01/02/1918	31/03/1918
Heading	War Diary D.A.D.O.S. 35th Divn Period 1st to 30th April 1918. Volume 2		
War Diary	In the field	01/04/1918	30/04/1918
Heading	War Diary. D.A.D. Ordce. 35th Divn. Period May 1st to 31st 1918. Volume II.		
War Diary	In the field	01/05/1918	05/05/1918
War Diary	Field	06/05/1918	30/06/1918
Heading	War Diary. D.A.D.O.S. 35 British Divn Period 1st to 31st July 1918. Volume. 2		
War Diary	Field	01/07/1918	31/08/1918
Heading	War Diary. D.A.D.O.S. 35th Brit Divn Period Sept 1st to 30th 1918. Volume II.		
War Diary	Field	01/09/1918	30/09/1918
Miscellaneous	Principal items of work done in the Divl Workshops during the Month of Septr.		
Heading	War Diary D.A.D.O.S. 35 Brit Divn Period 1st to 31st Octr. 1918. Volume 2		
War Diary	Field	01/10/1918	31/10/1918
Miscellaneous	The following are the principle terms of work performed in my shop during the month of October 1918		
Heading	War Diary. D.A.D.O.S. 35 British Divn. Period Nov 1st to 30th 1918. Volume 2		
War Diary		01/11/1918	24/11/1918
War Diary	Field	24/11/1918	30/11/1918

Heading	War Diary. D.A.D.O.S. 35th But Divn. Period. Dec 1st to 31st 1918. Volume 2		
War Diary	Field	01/12/1918	30/12/1918
Heading	War Diary D.A.D.O.S. 35th British Divn. Period 1st to 31st Jany 1919. Volume. 2		
War Diary	Field	01/01/1919	31/01/1919
War Diary	Tilques	01/02/1919	28/02/1919
Heading	War Diary. D.A.D.O.S. 35th Division. For Period. March 1st to 31st 1919. Volume 2		
War Diary	Tilques	01/03/1919	31/03/1919

WO95/2473
35 Div
Mar '16 - Apr '19
Dep. Ass. Director Ordnance
Service

(2)

35TH DIVISION
DIVL TROOPS

D. A. D. ORDNANCE SERVICES
MAR 1916-APR 1919

DADOS
35 D
Vol 1

War Diary

DADOS 35th Division

March 1916

Lawakton Slover
Lieut
DADOS 35th Division

Ap 19

WAR DIARY
or
INTELLIGENCE SUMMARY

(Erase heading not required.)

Army Form C. 2118

Instructions regarding War Diaries and Intelligence Summaries are contained in F. S. Regs., Part II. and the Staff Manual respectively. Title Pages will be prepared in manuscript.

Place	Date	Hour	Summary of Events and Information	Remarks and references to Appendices
	2.3.16		Lieut Williams left to take over duties of DADOS 19th Division	Laws
	5.3.16		Lieut L.A.S. Stover Jones to assume duties of DADOS 35 Divn	Laws
	7.3.16		Major T.H. Buller handed over to Lieut L.A.S Stover and left to assume duties of O.O. 1st Corps Troops	Laws
	12.3.16		150 Steel helmets arrived from Base	Laws
	13.3.16		1500 " " " "	Laws
	15.3.16		400 " " " "	Laws
	16.3.16		Conference of Armourers held at office by A.D.O.S to discuss question on Ordnance Services	Laws
	16.3.16		Orders received to issue the second Pat Helmet for officers and men. 20,030 demanded in Bulk from the Base	Laws

Army Form C. 2118

WAR DIARY
or
INTELLIGENCE SUMMARY
(Erase heading not required.)

Instructions regarding War Diaries and Intelligence Summaries are contained in F. S. Regs., Part II. and the Staff Manual respectively. Title Pages will be prepared in manuscript.

Place	Date	Hour	Summary of Events and Information	Remarks and references to Appendices
	19.3.16	8	Muzzle Diverting mountings arrived. Issued 1 each to 104 & 105 Inf. Bdes	Lewis
	20.3.16	17.150	O.R. Helmets arrived and issued	Lewis
	21.3.16		Notified that Battalions were being issued with 2 additional Lewis guns each	Lewis
	23.3.16	3060	O.R. Helmets arrived and issued	Lewis
	24.3.16	26	Lewis Guns received. Issued 2 to each Infantry Battalion	Lewis
	26.3.16		Went to rent Offices and Storehouses at Pas St. Maur vacated by Bn. H.Q. 6th Division	Lewis
	30.3.16	200	Steel Helmets arrived from Pas	Lewis
	31.3.16	8	Vickers Guns received from Pas. Issued 1 each to 105 & 106 Inf.Y. Bde. Issued 4 to 106 Brigade and 1 to 19 Northumberland Fusiliers	Lewis
		5	Muzzle Diverting Mountings arrived.	Lewis

Lauralson Never

Bn.O.O.S 35th Division

Army Form C. 2118

DADOS
35 Div

WAR DIARY
or
INTELLIGENCE SUMMARY
(Erase heading not required.)

Instructions regarding War Diaries and Intelligence Summaries are contained in F.S. Regs., Part II. and the Staff Manual respectively. Title Pages will be prepared in manuscript.

Place	Date	Hour	Summary of Events and Information	Remarks and references to Appendices
	1/1/16		1 Hotchkiss Gun received and allotted to Divl Cavalry. 5 Sets of "Dayfield" Protectors for Bombers received	Laws
	2/1/16		200 Steel Helmets received	Laws
	3/1/16		DADOS 1st Army called with reference to the return of Winter clothing	Laws
	6/1/16		750 Steel Helmets received. ADOS 1st Corps called. Proceeded with him to enquire at the inspection of vehicles on charge of Divl Amm Colt 550 Steel Helmets received	Laws
	10/1/16			Laws
	11/1/16		16 Hand bombs received from 1st Army Hy Mobile Workshop & issued to Trench Mortar Batteries 105 Infy Brigade	Laws
	14/1/16		3 - 2" Mortars received from Base	Laws

VGL

WAR DIARY
or
INTELLIGENCE SUMMARY
(Erase heading not required.)

Army Form C. 2118

Instructions regarding War Diaries and Intelligence Summaries are contained in F. S. Regs., Part II. and the Staff Manual respectively. Title Pages will be prepared in manuscript.

Place	Date	Hour	Summary of Events and Information	Remarks and references to Appendices
	16/10		6 - 9 cwt Wales received from Base	hand p
	18/10		750 Steel Helmets received	hand p
	19/10		Work Officer to new officers and Storehouses at Worville	hand p
	20/10		250 Steel Helmets received	hand p
			ADOS 1st Army visited Storehouses	
	23/10		4 Hand loads for Trench Mortar Batteries received from Heavy Artillery	hand p
			Workshop	
	25/10		600 Steel Helmets received from Base	hand p
	27/10		450 " " " " "	hand p
	28/10		1600 " " " " "	hand p
			ADOS 1st Corps with Colonel Anderson	hand p
			visited Office and inspected books and records	
	30/10		5640 Steel Helmets for Divisional Reserve received from the Base	hand p

Lawson Sloner
ADOS 35th Division

1875 Wt. W593/826 1,000,000 4/15 J R.C.&A. A.D.S.S./Forms/C 2118.

DADOS
Army Form C. 2118
25-D-3 Vol 3

WAR DIARY
or
INTELLIGENCE SUMMARY
(Erase heading not required.)

Instructions regarding War Diaries and Intelligence Summaries are contained in F. S. Regs., Part II. and the Staff Manual respectively. Title Pages will be prepared in manuscript.

Place	Date	Hour	Summary of Events and Information	Remarks and references to Appendices
K.S.4	4.5.16		1000 Steel Helmets received from Base	haw/s
	5.5.16		3 "Sea Hyem" Bomb Throwers received from 33rd Division	haw/s
	9.5.16		1000 Steel Helmets received from Base. 2pos 11" Infn Mortar started office with Personnel Arms & Equipt at the front ready & system of accounting for Stores at the Base. 1000 Steel Helmets received from Base	haw/s
	12.5.16		A pos 11" Infn called in about Carts for Trench Mortar Batteries	haw/s
	13.5.16		10 rds pack Ammn Wagons and Limbers to began to receive drawn to 35th Heavy Battery RGA	haw/s
	14.5.16		1200 Steel Helmets received from the Base	haw/s
	16.5.16		1000 do do do	haw/s
	20.5.16			
	21.5.16		4 - 3 Inch Stokes Mortars received and issued to 106/ Trench Mortar Battery	haw/s

1875 Wt. W593/826 1,000,000 4/15 T.B.C. & A. A.D.S.S./Forms/C. 2118.

Army Form C. 2118

WAR DIARY
or
INTELLIGENCE SUMMARY

(Erase heading not required.)

Instructions regarding War Diaries and Intelligence Summaries are contained in F.S. Regs., Part II. and the Staff Manual respectively. Title Pages will be prepared in manuscript.

Place	Date	Hour	Summary of Events and Information	Remarks and references to Appendices
	24.5.16		Lieut. Roberts D.A.D.O.S. 61st Division called in reference to mechanical work to be done on airplane 3.5" Stokes regarding Ordnance Services	Laws
	26.5.16		A.D.O.S. II Corps called	Laws
	29.5.16		100 Steel Helmets arrived from the Base	Laws
	30.5.16		4 – 3 inch Stokes Mortars received from the Base and issued to the O.C. 106th Trench Mortar Battery	Laws

C. Awdrin Plower
Capt.
D.A.D.O.S.
35th Div.

Army Form C. 2118

DADOS 35 DN

VOL 4

WAR DIARY
or
INTELLIGENCE SUMMARY
(Erase heading not required.)

Instructions regarding War Diaries and Intelligence Summaries are contained in F. S. Regs, Part II. and the Staff Manual respectively. Title Pages will be prepared in manuscript.

Place	Date	Hour	Summary of Events and Information	Remarks and references to Appendices
In the field	6/6/16	8—	3" Stokes Mortars received from O.O. 11th Corps Troops	
	7/6/16	1500	Steel Helmets received from Loo Kalas	
	16/6/16	4—	3" Stokes Mortars received from O.O. 11th Corps Troops	
			Moved Office and Stores to Busnes	
	16/6/16	4—	3" Stokes Mortars received from O.O. 11th Corps Troops	
	20/6/16		Have completed all Light Trench Mortar Batteries to Scale of 4 each.	
			Inspected clothing & equipment of Divisional units whilst refilling	
			— do — — do — — do — — do —	
	21/6/16		— do — — do — — do — — do —	
	29/6/16		ADOS 11th Corps called regarding issue of 4000 Cardigans	
			G.O.C. Division visited Storehouse and ordered 4000 Cardigans to be ordered. Many units incomplete through not maintaining scale of Summer clothing.	

WAR DIARY
or
INTELLIGENCE SUMMARY

Army Form C. 2118

(Erase heading not required.)

Instructions regarding War Diaries and Intelligence Summaries are contained in F. S. Regs., Part II. and the Staff Manual respectively. Title Pages will be prepared in manuscript.

Place	Date	Hour	Summary of Events and Information	Remarks and references to Appendices
In the Field	22/6/16		Attended conference held by a DOS 11th Corps to discuss Ordnance service in the event of a forward move, lecturer inspecting clothing etc.	
	23/6/16		200 Steel Helmets received from Base	
	24/6/16		300 " " " " "	
	25/6/16		Samples known anti-issue of ground Lathes for smoke helmets	
	29/6/16		DADOS 1st Army called re change of Bulleheads etc 19 Steel Bowls for Trench Mortar Batteries received. All Batteries now complete	
	30/6/16		Visited all Inf.y Bde Head Quarters regarding the handing over of old and surplus Ordnance Stores to Bde Salvage Officers	

[signature] Laurie Shaw
Captain
D.A.D.O.S 35th Division

35 July
3/35DS Army Form C. 2118
DADOS

Vol 5

WAR DIARY
or
INTELLIGENCE SUMMARY
(Erase heading not required.)

Instructions regarding War Diaries and Intelligence Summaries are contained in F. S. Regs., Part II. and the Staff Manual respectively. Title Pages will be prepared in manuscript.

Place	Date	Hour	Summary of Events and Information	Remarks and references to Appendices
	1-7-16		Instructed by ADOS 1st Army to demand 26 Lewis Guns to complete Division to scale of 8 per Battalion	laus?
	2-7-16		500 Steel Helmets received from Base	laus?
	3-7-16		Went to Poullens under ADOS 5th Corps	laus?
	4-7-16		Visited ADOS 5th Corps to discuss certain departmental matters	laus?
	5-7-16		26 Lewis Guns received from Base and issued. Battn? now complete with 8 each	laus?
	7-7-16		Went to new offices and stockrooms at Rue ... - Paris	laus?
	10-7-16		Went to new offices and stockrooms at Coursay	laus?
	11-7-16		ADOS 1st Corps called, re Guns, rifles Guns & mules in Jamaica ... of units of Division	laus?
	13-7-16		Went to Montanamt	laus?
	16-7-16		ADOS 15th Corps called and discussed various departmental matters	laus?
	17-7-16		Visited ADOS 15th Corps on the question of underclothing for Division	laus?

WAR DIARY
or
INTELLIGENCE SUMMARY

(Erase heading not required.)

Army Form C. 2118

Instructions regarding War Diaries and Intelligence Summaries are contained in F.S. Regs., Part II. and the Staff Manual respectively. Title Pages will be prepared in manuscript.

Place	Date	Hour	Summary of Events and Information	Remarks and references to Appendices
	19/7/16		Salvage officer reports for duty under me. Commenced collection and evacuation of ammo boxes & empty A.D. 15pr cases	haust
	20/7/16		25 Lewis Gun stand rests arrived from the base	haust
	21/6 22/7		Salvage work continued. Large quantities of stores evacuated to base	haust
	23/7/16		Large demands from all units received for stores & replaces losses in action	haust
	24/7		do	haust
	25/7/16		D.A.C. wired urgently for 30 Running out springs. Waited A.O.S. of he could supply	haust
	26/7/16		Buses 22 running out springs from 60 13" Corps Groups & delivered to D.A.C. by car	haust
	28/7/16		1000 Steel Helmets received from Base. Only 413 now required to complete entire issue of Officers and men	haust

Army Form C. 2118

WAR DIARY
or
INTELLIGENCE SUMMARY
(Erase heading not required.)

Instructions regarding War Diaries and Intelligence Summaries are contained in F. S. Regs., Part II. and the Staff Manual respectively. Title Pages will be prepared in manuscript.

Place	Date	Hour	Summary of Events and Information	Remarks and references to Appendices
In the Field	29/6 to 31/6		Large Quantities of Stores returned to Lent to Base which includes 1691 Rifles. 1336 Bayonets. 253,000 Rds S.A.A. 13796 18/pr Empty Cases.	Laws Q
			Following Guns and Vehicles have been replaced during the month	
			Ordnance Q.F. 15pr — 1	
			Guns Lewis — 303 — 13	
			" Vickers 303 — 3	
			Carts Salt Tank — 7	
			Travelling Kitchens Complete — 2	
			" Kitchens Door Portion — 3	
			" " Hind Portion — 1	Laws Q
			Wagons) Complete — 2	
			Limbered) Hind Portion — 1	
			G S) Door do — 1	
			Wagons Limbered R.E.	
			— do — do — Door Portion — 1	
			Wagons GS Mark X — 2	
			Gas officers used — 1	

Laurelson Shoes
CAPT.,
D.A.D.O.S. 35TH. DIVISION.

WAR DIARY
or
INTELLIGENCE SUMMARY
(Erase heading not required.)

Army Form C. 2118
35 / DADOS Vol 6

Place	Date	Hour	Summary of Events and Information	Remarks and references to Appendices
	1/7/16		304 Revolvers received from the Base for the rearming of Lewis Gunners	cont⁰
	3/7/16		Moved offices and stores to Corbie	cont⁰
	5/7/16		Moved to Carillon. 75 Hand Carts for Lewis Guns received from Base	cont⁰
	6/7/16		Sent S.T. Potter A.D.O. joined for temporary duty and assumed 100 Magazines Lewis Gun received.	cont⁰
	7/7/16		9 Hand Carts Lewis Gun received, which completes 12 each Battns to 15	cont⁰
	8/7/16		9 No 14 Periscopes received and march 15 was complete to Peake vide G.R.O. 861	cont⁰
	10/7/16		Moved to Warlancourt. 3 No 14 Periscopes received	cont⁰
	11/7/16		ADOS 18th Corps called and discussed several departmental troubles	cont⁰

Army Form C. 2118

WAR DIARY
or
INTELLIGENCE SUMMARY
(Erase heading not required.)

Instructions regarding War Diaries and Intelligence Summaries are contained in F. S. Regs., Part II. and the Staff Manual respectively. Title Pages will be prepared in manuscript.

Place	Date	Hour	Summary of Events and Information	Remarks and references to Appendices
In the Field	13/6		500 P.H.C. Helmets received. 1st consignment towards completing certain units to scale of one for officer and man	Churs 50
	17/6		Moved to new depot at Citadel	Churs
	18/6		1300 P.H.G Helmets received	Cans
	19/6		500 do do	Cans
	21/6		1500 do do. also 26 boxes 30'×30 for anti gas dumps	Cans
			3rd Div't artillery attached for Ordnance services	Cans
	24/6		500 P.H.G Helmets received	Cans
	26/6		Moved to Forked Tree. 500 P.H.G. Helmets received	Cans
	28/6		3rd Divt artillery transferred to 20th Division for Ordnance Services	Cans

WAR DIARY
or
INTELLIGENCE SUMMARY

Army Form C. 2118

(Erase heading not required.)

Instructions regarding War Diaries and Intelligence Summaries are contained in F. S. Regs., Part II. and the Staff Manual respectively. Title Pages will be prepared in manuscript.

Place	Date	Hour	Summary of Events and Information	Remarks and references to Appendices
	29/10		Move to Doullens. 35 Ord Artillery Coy mainly attached to Guards Div For Ordnance Services	Units
	30/10		Reports arrival etc to ADOS 6 Corps, 3rd Army	Cars
			Following Guns and Vehicles were issued during the month to replace losses, worn out etc	Cars
			Guns Lewis .303 — 4	
			" Vickers .303 — 4	
			Ordnance QF 18pdr — 3	
			Carriage, Field QF 18pdr — do — 1	
			Wagons amm QF 18pdr — 1	
			Limber wagon amm QF 18pdr — 1	
			Wagons GS MKX — 1	
			Kitchens Travelling complete (Body) — 1	
			Cars Officers Mess Tank — 1	Carl Mower Capt DADOS 35th Division

J. H. Bell

BS' Vol 7
Army Form C. 2118

BS/DADOS

WAR DIARY
or
INTELLIGENCE SUMMARY

(Erase heading not required.)

Instructions regarding War Diaries and Intelligence Summaries are contained in F. S. Regs., Part II. and the Staff Manual respectively. Title Pages will be prepared in manuscript.

Place	Date	Hour	Summary of Events and Information	Remarks and references to Appendices
	1.9.16		Moved Base O.O. Stores etc to new depot at Duisans. Called on ADOS 6th Corps to report arrival in new area	Ann 8
	2.9.16		Work office staff to La Cauchy	Ann 8
	3.9.16		Work office staff to Duisans	Ann 8
	5.9.16		ADOS 6th Corps visited depot and inspected books issues	Ann 8
	6.9.16		166 Magazine Lewis Gun received from La Base	Ann 8
	7.9.16		DADOS 3rd Army called. Recommended extension of Ord armr shop	Ann 8
Field	9.9.16		ADOS 6th Corps called and reviewed outstanding demands	Ann 8
	10.9.16		Inspector of Arms called and inspected Ord Arm Shop Recommended	Ann 8
	12.9.16		with view the addition of extension of shop. Decided to apply for 3 additional Armourers and 2 Cycle Orders.	Ann 8
	13.9.16		Visited Base with the Inspector of Armourers to see LoS Regt Armourers where employed. Also visited 60th Rif Arms Shop	Ann 8

Army Form C. 2118

WAR DIARY
or
INTELLIGENCE SUMMARY
(Erase heading not required.)

Instructions regarding War Diaries and Intelligence Summaries are contained in F. S. Regs., Part II. and the Staff Manual respectively. Title Pages will be prepared in manuscript.

Place	Date	Hour	Summary of Events and Information	Remarks and references to Appendices
	14.9.16		750 P+G Helmets and 1200 Steel Helmets received from the Base	Cause
	15.9.16		Search inspection of Regtl Armrs Shop and Inspection of Armourers	Cause
	16.9.16		5000 Blankets received as first consignment of winter issue	Cause
	17.9.16		7000 P&G Helmets received from the Base	Cause
	18.9.16		Further 5000 Blankets received	Cause
	19.9.16		1068 Steel Helmets received	Cause
	20.9.16		3 additional Armrs and 2 Lewis Fitters deputed for duty. All Machine and Lewis Guns and bicycles to be overhauled in Armr Shop. D.R.O. published. All rounds of bicycles to be controlled by Armr	Cause
	21.9.16		Base Boot Repair Shop opened for use by units who have no qualified shoemaker	Cause
	22.9.16		A.D.O.S. called to review outstanding demands. 10000 each shirts and Socks received from the Base. Special consignment	Cause

WAR DIARY
or
INTELLIGENCE SUMMARY

Army Form C. 2118

Place	Date	Hour	Summary of Events and Information	Remarks and references to Appendices
	25.9.16		DDOS 3rd Army visits Depot and inspects	Init'd
	26.9.16		2500 O.A.G. Helmets received from Base. Division now complete to scale of one per officer and men	Init'd
	27.9.16		Visited ADOS 6th Corps also Div Baths and Salvage Dump	Init'd
	28.9.16		Visited the 3rd Div D.Q. to interview Staff Captain	Init'd

30/9/16

C. Awdson Plüner
Captain
DADOS 35th Division

WAR DIARY or INTELLIGENCE SUMMARY

Army Form C. 2118

35/ DADOS Vol 9

Place	Date	Hour	Summary of Events and Information	Remarks and references to Appendices
	14/10		Visited D.O.C. 106th Infy Bde re formation of a Brigade Laundry	Cont'd
	15/10		Board of Enquiry of 1st met reassembled. Visited DADOS 49th Divn with reference to stores for 33rd Divl Artillery	Cont'd
	16/10		Meeting of Qr Master & AMLO's. AAC & MS provided. Division complete with Telescopic Sights Rifles.	Cont'd
	17/10		ADOS 6th Corps called, viewfacts infront a/c etc. 1173 Magazines Lewis Gun received from the Base.	Cont'd
	19/10		Divl Trench Mortar officer called with reference to 2 inch Mortars out of action. Arms Repairs of Lee Enfield mechanism issued to and got 6 from Heavy Mobile Workshop. Delivered Men by car at 9.0 h.	Cont'd
	20/10		Issued a further 6 Lee Enfield mechanism from Heavy Mobile Shop desired to Divl Trench Mortar officer. All guns in action again	Cont'd
	22/10		D.D.O.S. 3rd Army with the DADOS 6th C. visited the rept. shops and salvage dumps	Cont'd

Army Form C. 2118

WAR DIARY
or
INTELLIGENCE SUMMARY
(Erase heading not required.)

Instructions regarding War Diaries and Intelligence Summaries are contained in F. S. Regs., Part II. and the Staff Manual respectively. Title Pages will be prepared in manuscript.

Place	Date	Hour	Summary of Events and Information	Remarks and references to Appendices
In the Field	1/10		A. a. a. Only held a meeting of Q. Masters & QmSgt. to discuss Ordnance question especially the need for economy	[initials]
	2/10		10,000 Vests received from the Base as 1st consignment of winter clothing	[initials]
	3/10		D.D.O.S. 3rd Army visited Depot, Shops & Salvage Dump	[initials]
	7/10		Prepared for the G.O.C. a Special Statement of all issues of clothing etc made to 16th H.C.S since the Batt came overseas.	[initials]
	9/10		Visited H.Q. 106th Bde	[initials]
	10/10		Inspected with the A.D.O.S. 104 m/c Guns or No 3 Section 35 D.A.C.	[initials]
	12/10		Inspected Laundries of the 104th & 105th Brigades	[initials]
	13/10		1183 Steel Helmets received from the Base this confirms issues to scale of 1 per Officer & man vide G.R.O. 1847	[initials]
	14/10		Inspected Clothing, Boots & Equipt of No 3 Section 35 D.A.C. Found Lewis Gun Lock in condition of Lewis Gun in charge of 18 H.K.S.	[initials]

1875 Wt. W593/826 1,000,000 11/17 J.B.C. & A. A.D.S.S./Forms/C. 2118.

Army Form C. 2118

WAR DIARY
or
INTELLIGENCE SUMMARY
(Erase heading not required.)

Instructions regarding War Diaries and Intelligence Summaries are contained in F. S. Regs., Part II. and the Staff Manual respectively. Title Pages will be prepared in manuscript.

Place	Date	Hour	Summary of Events and Information	Remarks and references to Appendices
	24/10		21,000 drawers woollen and 9,000 vests received from the Base. Completed issues with these articles	Appx
	25/10		1st consignment of three things & under clothing received from the Base	Appx
	26/10		12,000 2nd Blankets drawn from OC 3rd Army Troops No 3	Appx
	29/10		G.O.C. 35th Division inspected Depots & Workshops. Visited 106th Inf Bde H.Q.	Appx
	30/10		Inspected Q.M. Stores 17th R Scots. Visited 105th Inf Bde H.Q.	Appx
			Following Guns etc were repaired during the month	
			3" Trench Mortars 3	
			2" " " 1	
			Ord Q.F 4.5" How" 2	
			do 18 pdr 1	
			Guns Lewis 1	

Laurentin Martin
Cooper
DADOS 35th Division

1875 Wt. W593/826 1,000,000 4/17 T.R.C. & A. A.D.S.S./Forms/C. 2118. 3/1/10

War Diary / Intelligence Summary — Army Form C. 2118

D.A.D.O.S. 35 War Diary Sr. (Orgwi) 1-11-16 to 30-11-16. Vol 9

Place	Date	Hour	Summary of Events and Information	Remarks and references to Appendices
	1/11		Conference of QR Masters held in office. RAOR supply forwarded. Inspected clothing & equipment of 20th Coy Divl Train.	[aust]
	2/11		– do – – do – of 17th R. Scots	[aust]
	3/11		– do – – do – of M.T. Coy No. 2 & 3 Coys A.S.C. Train & 18th L. & S.	[aust]
	4/11		– do – – do – of 26th & 23rd Manc Regt, 105th M/c Gun Coy & 26th 15 Divisional	[aust]
	5/11		– do – – do – remainder of 23rd Manc Regt & 15th Notts & Derbys	[aust]
	6/11		D.A.D.O.S. 3rd Army called. Inspected Shops etc & also received recruits of units of the 104th Bde.	[aust]
	7/11		Inspected clothing & equipt of "A" & "D" 151st Bde R.F.A. at Sayers. "B" 157th Bde at Battery H.Q. also 17th Lancs Fusiliers	[aust]
	8/11		Inspected clothing & equipt of 35th Supply Column & 15/159 Bde to 7s.	[aust]
	9/11		– do – – do – of 106th Bde Ambce Compd & 105th M/c Gun Coy	[aust]
	10/11		– do – – do – No 2 & 4 sections 35 D.A.C, Camp Comdrs stores & 20 L. Sun depot at Sourghot. Inspected transport section of 205th & D.O.H. Decond of 106th Bde & Laundry	[aust]
In the Field	11/11		– do – Enter visited depot det 6 106th Bde & Laundry. Inspected transport section of 205th & D.O.H. Decond of 106th Bde & Laundry & 695 RE	[aust]
Do	12/11		Completed inspections of D.O.H. Decond Coy R.E. and A, C & D Batteries 157th Bde R.F.A.	[aust]

WAR DIARY
or
INTELLIGENCE SUMMARY
(Erase heading not required.)

Army Form C. 2118

Place	Date	Hour	Summary of Events and Information	Remarks and references to Appendices
	13th		Inspected Clothing & Equipt of A B C & D Batteries 158th RFA and 18th Lancs Divn (26th)	[Ans 1]
	14th		do — do — 104th M/ca Gun Coy — completed 20th & 205th Infant Co RE	[Ans 2]
	15th		— do — do — of Transport men 14th Gloucesters.	[Ans 3]
	16th		— do — Fortnightly conference of Q. M's held under presidency of A A & Q M G.	[Ans 4]
	17th		Large consignment of Winter Clothing received from Base.	[Ans 5]
			Inspected Clothing & Equipt of men in wagon lines of TB "C" 151st Bde R.F.A.	
	18th		— do — do — of Transport men 104th M/co Gun Coy	[Ans 6]
	19th		— do — do — of Wagon line men of "D" 151st Bde	[Ans 7]
	21st		— do — Men of "F" L Gro (completed this unit)	[Ans 8]
	22nd		— do — of 16th Cheshire Regt and transport men of 205th Inft Co RE.	[Ans 9]
	24th		— do — Armoury 2 Coys 15th Lancs Divn also 14th Gloucester Regt	[Ans 10]

Army Form C. 2118

WAR DIARY
or
INTELLIGENCE SUMMARY
(Erase heading not required.)

Instructions regarding War Diaries and Intelligence Summaries are contained in F. S. Regs., Part II. and the Staff Manual respectively. Title Pages will be prepared in manuscript.

Place	Date	Hour	Summary of Events and Information	Remarks and references to Appendices
	26/6		ADS 3rd Army visited Depot. Steps taken to report 16,720 Small Bore Respirators received from the Base	Cont'd
	27/6		Deputation of Staff Officers from 3rd Army Staff Officers School visited the depot for a tour of inspection. Sent three specially to 3rd Army heavy mobile workshop for 12 Lee Enfield Mechanisms for 8" Trench Mortars	Cont'd
	29/6		Received 84 Lewis Guns to complete Infantry Battalion (less Drums) to scale of 10 Lewis Guns per Batt.	Cont'd
	30/6		2650 Small Bore Respirators received from Base (3rd RA) Inspected locality & equipt. of Transport men of 15 Sherwood Foresters	Cont'd

(. Awalsin Muir)
Captain
ADS 35th Division

WAR DIARY
or
INTELLIGENCE SUMMARY

(Erase heading not required.)

Army Form C. 21..

Instructions regarding War Diaries and Intelligence Summaries are contained in F.S. Regs., Part II. and the Staff Manual respectively. Title Pages will be prepared in manuscript.

Place	Date	Hour	Summary of Events and Information	Remarks and references to Appendices
Lille Deck	1/10/14		Conference of Or Master held at AA & QmG. DAQS of Korps called re handing over of Korps. Reserves etc	[inits]
	2/10/14		Visited new depot at Bethune to arrange erection of storehouses	[inits]
	3/10/14		Commenced move to new depot. Visited over new Reserves etc	[inits]
	4/10/14		DAQS of Division	[inits]
	5/10/14		DAQS of Division called re attached troops etc	[inits]
	6/10/14		34.00 Small Box Respirators received. Visited new refilling points.	[inits]
	7/10/14		DQGS 3rd Army called	[inits]
	8/10/14		Visits OC 14th Gloucesters to discuss Ordnance questions	[inits]
	9/10/14		Visited OC 15th HLI 5 & 11th R Scots do — do — do —	[inits]
	10/10/14		DAQS 3rd Army re fester new depot	[inits]
	11/10/14		Visited all OCs 104th Brigade to discuss Ordnance question	[inits]

1875 Wt. W593/826 1,000,000 4/15 T.R.C. & A. A.D.S.S./Forms/C. 2118.

Army Form C. 2118

WAR DIARY
or
INTELLIGENCE SUMMARY
(Erase heading not required.)

Place	Date	Hour	Summary of Events and Information	Remarks and references to Appendices
	1/10/15		Conference of O. Medls held at HQ. 1 Indiv.	[initials]
	2/10/15		DADOS 1 Div called & to bring over of 10 pr. Reserve etc	[initials]
	3/10/15		Visited new depot at Bellecourt. to arrange issues of Ordnance	[initials]
	4/10/15		Government ment to new depot. Handed over new Reserve to	[initials]
	5/10/15		DADOS 1 Divisn	[initials]
	6/10/15		DADOS 1 Divisn called to attend conference	[initials]
	7/10/15		The Indn Div Reginals Board. Visited new refilling point.	[initials]
	8/10/15		DDOS 3rd Army called.	[initials]
	9/10/15		Visited OC 1st Gloucesters to arrange Ordnance Turnovers	[initials]
	10/10/15		Visited OC 15th MGS & 1st R.Scots & gave ... to —	[initials]
	11/10/15		DDOS 3rd Army inspected new depot	[initials]
	12/10/15		Visited all OCs 10th Bde to discuss Ordnance question	[initials]

WAR DIARY
or
INTELLIGENCE SUMMARY

Army Form C. 2118

D.A.D.O.S

Vol 10

Place	Date	Hour	Summary of Events and Information	Remarks and references to Appendices
In the Field	15/10/16		Visited G.O.C. 106th Infy Bde on Ordnance matters	cont
	16/10/16		Inspected Kent & B.B.S. Laundries & Baths. 1000 Small Box Respirators received	cont
	17/10/16		A.D.O.S. VI Corps called re Boxrespts and Anti Gas appliances. 2,500 Small Box Respirators received	cont
	18/10/16		attended conference at H.Q VI Corps held by A.D.O.S. VI Corps	cont
	19/10/16		Visited G.O.C. 105th Infy Bde on Ordnance matters. Balance of Small Box Respirators to complete WE received. Issue proceeding	cont
			troops in rest area	
	20/10/16		A.D.O.S. VI Corps called re additional armourers for use arms (Coy)	cont
	24/10/16		D.D.O.S. 3rd Army called	cont

J.A Watson Muir Captn
D.A.D.O.S. 35th Division

31/10/16

Army Form C. 2118

WAR DIARY
or
INTELLIGENCE SUMMARY
(Erase heading not required.)

Instructions regarding War Diaries and Intelligence Summaries are contained in F.S. Regs., Part II. and the Staff Manual respectively. Title Pages will be prepared in manuscript.

Place	Date	Hour	Summary of Events and Information	Remarks and references to Appendices
In the field	14/10/16		Visited G.O.C. 106th Inf.y Bde re Ordnance matters	[init]
	16/10/16		Inspected 100th Bde Laundries & Baths. Hood small Bot Respirators received	[init]
	17/10/16		A.D.O.S. VI Corps called re Blankets and Anti Gas appliances. 2500 small Bot Respirators received	[init]
	18/10/16		Attended conference at A.G. VI Corps held re A.D.O.S. VI Corps	[init]
	19/10/16		Visited G.O.C. 105th Inf.y Bde re Ordnance matters. Balance of small Bot Respirators to complete 10% reserve issued. Issue proceeded to units in rest area	[init]
	20/10/16		A.D.O.S. VI Corps called re additional armourers for Bde arms (Lt)	[init]
	21/10/16		A.D.O.S. 3rd Army called	[init]

J.A. Watson Major
D.A.D.O.S. 35th Division

31/10/16

WAR DIARY
or
INTELLIGENCE SUMMARY

(Erase heading not required.)

Army Form C. 2118

DADOS Vol XI

Place	Date	Hour	Summary of Events and Information	Remarks and references to Appendices
In Field	1/7		Visited GOC 10th Div's also BRA. attended conference at Divl HQ. and hear by the ADOS	MGNS
	2/7		Visited BRA. HQ a. 10th Divl Train and GOC 10th Div's to discuss certain Ordnance questions. Inspected Salvage Dump	Laws
	3/7		200-Body Shields and 200 Silk Pickets received for protection of Shrapnel operators.	Laws
	4/7		Specimen Ground Sheet converted for use as Mackintosh received, inspected by Brigr M Division Junl	Laws
	6/7		DADOS 3rd Army and DADOS Quarto Divisions called to inspect Report Books etc	Laws
Div	6/7		Visited BRA. regarding new reorganisation of Divl artillery and discussed	Laws
	9/7		Visited DDOS 3rd army	Laws
	11/7		GOC 35th Division inspected Regtl Storehouses shops etc	Laws

WAR DIARY
or
INTELLIGENCE SUMMARY

(Erase heading not required.)

Army Form C. 2118

Instructions regarding War Diaries and Intelligence Summaries are contained in F. S. Regs., Part II. and the Staff Manual respectively. Title Pages will be prepared in manuscript.

Place	Date	Hour	Summary of Events and Information	Remarks and references to Appendices
Dr. H. E. Leek	1/7		Visited GOC 104th Bde, also G.R.A. Attended conference at 11 Corps. Dined at Mess of the A.D.O.S.	W
	2/7		Visited G.R.A. H & 60 Pdr Train and GOC 106th Bde to discuss certain ordnance matters. Inspected salvage dump.	W
	3/7		200 Body Shields and 200 S.A.A. Jackets received for protection against shrapnel splinters.	W
	4/7		Specimen Ground sheet, converted for use as Mackintosh received. Issued to 19th N. Division for trial.	W
	5/7		D.A.D.O.S. 31st Army and D.D.O.S. Guards Division called to inspect report books etc.	W
	6/7		Visited G.R.A. regarding new arrangements of MG artillery & D.L.	W
	9/7		Visited D.D.O.S. 31st Army	W
	11/7		G.O.C. 35th Division inspected rept. disciplinary duties etc	W

WAR DIARY
or
INTELLIGENCE SUMMARY

Army Form C. 2118

(Erase heading not required.)

Instructions regarding War Diaries and Intelligence Summaries are contained in F.S. Regs., Part II. and the Staff Manual respectively. Title Pages will be prepared in manuscript.

Place	Date	Hour	Summary of Events and Information	Remarks and references to Appendices
In the field	12/7		17 Lewis Guns received in part completion of 10 per Infantry Battn. excluding Pioneers	[ctd]
	14/7		ADOS 3rd Army called re training of armrs in care and upkeep of Lewis Gun. Proposed to be trained elsewhere.	[ctd]
	15/7		Attended conference at VI Corps H.Q. held by ADOS VI Corps. AOOS called at 10pm. en route for 3rd Army H.Q. to arr. 15gr. wanted for training	[ctd]
	16/7		Draft G.O. 106 Bn regarding sending more & new armrs dumps for ordnance stores	[ctd]
	17/7		Lorries for the Armd dept conference. 4 new armourers referred for training	[ctd]
	20/7		DADOS 55 Divn called. to inspect books shewing system adopted to deal with Pack Stores etc etc	[ctd]

Army Form C. 2118

WAR DIARY
or
INTELLIGENCE SUMMARY
(Erase heading not required.)

Instructions regarding War Diaries and Intelligence Summaries are contained in F. S. Regs., Part II. and the Staff Manual respectively. Title Pages will be prepared in manuscript.

Place	Date	Hour	Summary of Events and Information	Remarks and references to Appendices
	13th		1) Lewis Guns received on first consignment of 12 for Infantry Battn. exchanging Pioneers	[init]
	14th		D.A.D.O.S. 3rd Army called re turning of Arms in over and repair. Lewis Gun trm to be packed elsewhere.	[init]
	15th		Attended conference at VI Corps H.Q. held by A.D.O.S. VI Corps. A.D.O.S called at Depot. en route for 3rd Army H.Q. A Armr. Sgr. upgraded for training	[init]
	15th		D.A.D. Z.O. 106th Div. requesting information re news dumps for Ordnance stores	[init]
	16th		Issue to the Harm Lgts. confirmed. A new Armourers repaired for training	[init]
	20th		D.A.D.O.S 55th Divsn called to inspect tools showing system adopted to deal with small stores etc etc	[init]

1875 Wt. W593/826 1,000,000 4/15 J.B.C. & A. A.D.S.S./Forms/C. 2118.

Army Form C. 2118

WAR DIARY
or
INTELLIGENCE SUMMARY
(Erase heading not required.)

Instructions regarding War Diaries and Intelligence Summaries are contained in F. S. Regs., Part II. and the Staff Manual respectively. Title Pages will be prepared in manuscript.

Place	Date	Hour	Summary of Events and Information	Remarks and references to Appendices
In the Field	25/7		7 Lewis Guns received which completes all Infantry Battn. except Pioneers to 12 guns per Battn.	[init.]
	26/7		Rugs for all units arrived without blankets. Battn. very much in arrears of blankets for some obtained 1385 from OO 35 Army change. Two blankets per man Infantry reserve remains 2500 in addition. Troops not now suffering.	[init.]
	27/7		Received 2600 blankets from the Base	[init.]
	31/7		D.A.D.O.S. 58" Divn called. Left two sheep skin for 3 days trial for 35 Divn. in Infantry will observe closely in the system adopted by 35 Divn. Mark X. Guns and Vehicles replaced during the month. One M.G. 2" Trench Mortar 1- Lewis gun Saymrs. G.S. Mark X 1- Limbered by Jones II Centre	[init.]

Laurelson Munro
D.A.D.O.S. 35th Division

WAR DIARY
or
INTELLIGENCE SUMMARY
(Erase heading not required.)

Army Form C. 2118

Place	Date	Hour	Summary of Events and Information	Remarks and references to Appendices
In the Field	23/7		7 Lewis Guns received which completes all Infantry Battns except Pioneers to 12 guns per Battn	(cont.)
	24/7		Drafts for all units arrived without trouble. Obtained very much our strength. No blankets for issue. Obtained 1385 from O.O. 3rd Army. Troops sleeping as a temporary measure. Received 2500 in addition.	(cont.)
	25/7		Received 2500 Blankets from the Base.	(cont.)
	27/7		D.A.D.O.S. 58" Divn called, after his Bttys left for 3 days leaving 35 box for dealing with Ordnance Stores in the system adopted by 35th Divn. Guns and Vehicles replaced during the month. Ord M.G. 2" Trench Mortars. — 1. Wagon G.S. Mark X — 1 Limbered Gy Somme V Carts —	(cont.)

Laurelson Nugent
Ma.Gen 35th Division
Capt.

WAR DIARY
or
INTELLIGENCE SUMMARY

(Erase heading not required.)

Army Form C. 2118

DADos 182
Vol 15

Place	Date	Hour	Summary of Events and Information	Remarks and references to Appendices
	5/2/17		Attended conference held at HQ VI Corps by the A.D.O.S. Army officers of Battⁿ 10H B.A.C. also 17th R Div & 18th Div 9.	Cont
	6.2.17		Went Office to Doqueneau	Cont
	7.2.17		Went Stores Office to Vignacourt	Cont
	9.2.17		Attended conference held by G.O. at 10th Head Qrs	Cont
	11.2.17		Visited G.O. 10th Brigade re Boots for 23rd Maners	Cont
	13.2.17		Visited A.O.D.S. H Corps regarding move to Caix. Arrangements regarding Trench Plans for the Division	Cont
	15.2.17		Visited new area and fixed up Storehouses Shops etc	Cont
	17.2.17		Went Hd arms Shop to Caix	Cont
	18.2.17		Went Office & Stores to Caix	Cont

WAR DIARY
or
INTELLIGENCE SUMMARY

Army Form C. 2118

(Erase heading not required.)

Place	Date	Hour	Summary of Events and Information	Remarks and references to Appendices
In the field	5/3/17		Attended conference held at H.Q. 17 Corps by the A.D.M.S. Comdg officers of 104th DAC also 17th R Scots & 15th H.L.I.	Visitors (cont)
	6.3.17		Moved office to Bouquemaison	(cont)
	7.3.17		Moved office to Vignacourt	(cont)
	1.3.17		Attended conference held by D.D.M.S. XVII Corps about our probable move for 23rd March	(cont)
	2.3.17		Visited G.O.C. 104th Brigade re Dents for 23rd March	(cont)
	3.3.17		Visited A.D.M.S. 17 Corps regarding move to Corbie. Arrange matters regarding Trench Place for the Division	(cont)
	5.3.17		Visited new area and fixed up Advanced Dispatch etc	(cont)
	4.3.17		Moved Hors Amm? Pk &c to Corbie	(cont)
	6.3.17		Moved office & Hors to Corbie	(cont)

Army Form C. 2118

WAR DIARY
or
INTELLIGENCE SUMMARY
(Erase heading not required.)

Instructions regarding War Diaries and Intelligence Summaries are contained in F. S. Regs., Part II, and the Staff Manual respectively. Title Pages will be prepared in manuscript.

Place	Date	Hour	Summary of Events and Information	Remarks and references to Appendices
In the field	19/7		A.D.O.S. IV Corps and D.A.D.O.S. H. Lanka called and inspected shops and dept.	(an't)
	20/7		Visited G.O.C. 101 Bde re Gun Boots. Visited A.D.O.S. IV Corps re Trenches in Trench Stores. L.O.C. Trench Mortar L.O. Trench artillery visited Dept. shops etc and saw a demonstration with the Lewis Gun.	(an't)
	21/7		24 additional Lewis Guns received from Base. Issued 2 for practice making 14 in possession of 101 Bde except Pioneers.	(an't)
	22/7		Large consignments of Trench Stores received.	(an't)
	25/7		Heavy demands for Service Dress Clothing received from units a result of the appalling condition of the Trenches.	(an't)
	26/7		Held a conference with the A.D.M.S. as to best method of arranging for each man coming out of the line to be bathed & equipped with a complete set of clean underclothing, suit of service dress, and puttees. G.O.C. 35 Bde visited Dept. shops and offices	(an't)

Army Form C. 2118

WAR DIARY
or
INTELLIGENCE SUMMARY
(Erase heading not required.)

Instructions regarding War Diaries and Intelligence Summaries are contained in F. S. Regs., Part II. and the Staff Manual respectively. Title Pages will be prepared in manuscript.

Place	Date	Hour	Summary of Events and Information	Remarks and references to Appendices
In the Field	19/7/17		A.D.S. IV Corps and D.A.D.V.S. II Corps called and inspected Shops and Depot.	(App.1)
	20/7/17		Visited G.O.C. 10th Div. re Gun Boot. Visited A.D.O.S. IV Corps re Trench Stores. G.O.C. Trench War with C.O. Trench artillery visited Depot, Shops, etc and saw a demonstration with the Lewis Gun.	(App.2)
	21/7/17		24 additional Lewis Gun covers from D.A.C. Issued 2 for First Marking 14 in possession of Batt. Keeps Pioneer.	(App.3)
	22/7/17		Large consignments of Trench stores received	(App.4)
	25/7/17		Heavy demand for Service Dress clothing received from units on account of the appalling condition of the Trenches.	(App.5)
	26/7/17		Held a conference with the A.D.M.S. as to best method of arranging for each man coming out of the line to be better dressed with a complete set of clean underclothing, suit of service dress, and puttees. G.O.C. 35th Div. visited Depot, Shops and Offices.	(App.6)

WAR DIARY
or
INTELLIGENCE SUMMARY

Army Form C. 2118

Place	Date	Hour	Summary of Events and Information	Remarks and references to Appendices
	27/7		Visited G.S.C. 104 & 106th Bde. Made final arrangements for the opening of an Advanced A.D.S. intended to step Batt^n supplies into the lines. Also arrange final details of the opening of a Rest Refreshing & Cleaning Stop for Divis^l Infantry.	Nil
	28/7		Opened the Advanced A.D.S. Intended at 6 a.m. Visited A.D.S. IV Corps Refoné now arrival of stores from the Base which are now 5 days overdue.	Nil

Lansdown Sloter
CAPT.
D.A.D.O.S. 35TH DIVISION.

WAR DIARY
or
INTELLIGENCE SUMMARY

Army Form C. 2118

(Erase heading not required.)

In the Field

Place	Date	Hour	Summary of Events and Information	Remarks and references to Appendices
	27/7		Visited G/C 104 & 106th Bde. Made final arrangements for the opening of an advanced Armr Workshop to keep Batt" supplied with clean rifles. Also arrange final details of the opening of a Boot Repairing & Darning shop for 2 Bdes clothing	Appx
	28/7		Opened the Advanced Armr Workshop at 6 a.m. Visited ADOS IV Corps & reported non arrival of stores from the Base which are now 5 days overdue	Appx

Lauselou Hughes
CAPT.
D.A.D.O.S. 35th DIVISION.

WAR DIARY or INTELLIGENCE SUMMARY

D.A.D.O.S. 35th Div.

Army Form C. 2118

(Erase heading not required.)

Place	Date	Hour	Summary of Events and Information	Remarks and references to Appendices
In the Field	1-3-17		Started Div¹ cleaning and repairing shop for Service Dress clothing to equip men on leaving the trenches	[over?]
	2-3-17		Visited B.O. 104th, 105th and 106th Inf⁹ Bdes. also visited Advanced shop	[over?]
	6-3-17		Visited D.R.A. regarding Gun Boots and Ordnance matters generally	[over?]
	8-3-17		Visited H.Q. R.A.C. regarding Running out of Serge	[over?]
	9-3-17		Visited Staff Captains of Infantry Bdes re Trench Stores etc	[over?]
	10-3-17		Visited Advanced Ammunition shop also started an advanced salvage dump with ten men	[over?]
	12-3-17		Held a conference with the A.D.M.S. regarding undercutting of OvC Baths	[over?]
	13-3-17		12 Working Trench Jerkins received from Base and issued	[over?]
	14-3-17		Visited Labour to try and make arrangements for the salvage of the advanced area. Decided to ask "G" for permission to send	[over?]

Army Form C. 2118

WAR DIARY
or
INTELLIGENCE SUMMARY

(Erase heading not required.)

Instructions regarding War Diaries and Intelligence Summaries are contained in F. S. Regs., Part II. and the Staff Manual respectively. Title Pages will be prepared in manuscript.

Place	Date	Hour	Summary of Events and Information	Remarks and references to Appendices
	1.5.17		Staff met class and referring also for leave has closing Kingston in bring to time	[illegible]
	2.5.17		Visited 25th tail to and 26th Dept tail at work as usual Hot	[illegible]
	6.5.17		Notice took a running over road and Entrance near Peronne	[illegible]
	8.5.17		Note to tape again sniper orders	[illegible]
	9.5.17		Road Stop Engineer disposed large into two lines	[illegible]
	10.5.17		Visited Advance Amm. of Dp also Called in advance dump will be now	[illegible]
	12.5.17		Held a conference with the A.A.M.S. regarding ammunition also roads	[illegible]
	13.5.17		12 Monday truck received from Regne and Dump	[illegible]
	14.5.17		Wrote Letter to Hy and made arrangements for the shift the 3rd advance Am. Recorded and left "Hy" for Peronne [illegible]	[illegible]

1875 Wt. W593/826 1,900,000 4/15 J.B.C. & A. A.D.S.S./Forms/C. 2118.

Army Form C. 2118

WAR DIARY
or
INTELLIGENCE SUMMARY
(Erase heading not required.)

Place	Date	Hour	Summary of Events and Information	Remarks and references to Appendices
In the Field	17.3.17		Up a long tack day with some A.O.C. Officers. Went round mission as to different French areas not go into tent salvage dump.	Auto
			3 am'b slips sent on a refresher course in the repair and care of telescopic sights, Rifles and Binoculars, which in future will so far as possible be undertaken in the Newt Army Shop	Auto
	18.3.17		Head office depot to Rozières	Auto
	19.3.17		Visited D.O.Cs 104, 105 & 106 Inf Bdes also O.C 15" M.G. on Ordnance question	Auto
	20.3.17		G.O.C. 35 Division inspected Depot and Workshops	Auto
	21.3.17		Visited DADOS 32nd Division regarding the administration of 154th Brigade R.F.A.	Auto
	25.3.17		Arranged with DADOS 61st Division as to administration of 157" Bde R.F.A.	Auto

WAR DIARY
or
INTELLIGENCE SUMMARY
(Erase heading not required.)

Army Form C. 2118

Place	Date	Hour	Summary of Events and Information	Remarks and references to Appendices
In Field	17.3.17		Up to to-day with day with some A.C.C. alterations look place. Trainees as to disposal as an officers are heard a week not of the West Lahore dmk.	[illegible]
			3 new Lffs sent on a regular course in the Sufa and one of Telescopic sights type and Binoculars which is being left as far as is fancied to undertaken on next turn is Ship	[illegible]
	18.3.17		Head office orders to Rogers	[illegible]
	19.3.17		Visited S.o.S 104, 105 and 2nd offices and took HR to on Lahore Division	[illegible]
	20.3.17		G.O.C 35 Division inspected Rapur and Sialkot.	[illegible]
	21.3.17		Visited R.A.O.B.D. Division regarding the ammunition [illegible] Brigade R.F.A	[illegible]
	25.3.17		Arranged with Dates for Division as to ammunition [illegible] B.A.C R.F.A	[illegible]

Army Form C. 2118

WAR DIARY
or
INTELLIGENCE SUMMARY

(Erase heading not required.)

Instructions regarding War Diaries and Intelligence Summaries are contained in F. S. Regs., Part II. and the Staff Manual respectively. Title Pages will be prepared in manuscript.

Place: In the Field

Date	Hour	Summary of Events and Information	Remarks and references to Appendices
29.3.17		Moved Kept and Officer to Neola	Laos?
30.3.17		24 Lewis Guns received from the Base. All Battalions except (Pioneers) are now complete with 16 Lewis Guns each	Laos?

L. A. Walsh Nish
Capbean
D.A.D.O.S. 35th Division

31/3/17

1875 Wt. W593/826 1,000,000 4/15 T.R.C. & A. A.D.S.S./Forms/C. 2118.

Army Form C. 2118

WAR DIARY
or
INTELLIGENCE SUMMARY
(Erase heading not required.)

Instructions regarding War Diaries and Intelligence Summaries are contained in F. S. Regs., Part II. and the Staff Manual respectively. Title Pages will be prepared in manuscript.

Place	Date	Hour	Summary of Events and Information	Remarks and references to Appendices
In the Field	29.3.17		Record kept and offices to Neole all Battalion except	Laus?
	30.3.17		2H Coys have received for the base. 2H Coys are now comfort. all the Luis Gun in the Drancis) are not comfort here	Laus?

[signature] 3/3/17

L. A. Walton Rhoe
C. of S. 35th Division

1875 Wt. W593/826 1,000,000 4/15 T.R.C. & A. A.D.S.S./Forms/C. 2118.

Army Form C. 2118

WAR DIARY
or
INTELLIGENCE SUMMARY
(Erase heading not required.)

A.D.M.S. 35th Division

Place	Date	Hour	Summary of Events and Information	Remarks and references to Appendices
In the Field	3/7/17		ADMS & leaps visited Depot	July 1914
	12/7/17		Visit Depot, store dumps/shops & workshops to Mourly Lazache	
	15/7/17		A a D M S visited Depot & workshops	
	16/7/17		ADMS called regarding underclothing for 101st Battn.	
	17/7/17		Leaner Hole Depot of all French areas places	
	20/7/17		D.A.D.M.S. called about Lewis Trench	
	25/7/17		300 bell tents allotted to Division	
	28/7/17		A.D.M.S. visited Depot	

Lawrison Oliver
Captain
D.A.D.M.S. 35th Division

1875 Wt. W593/826 1,000,000 4/15 T.B.C. & A. A.D.S.S./Forms/C. 2118.

WAR DIARY
or
INTELLIGENCE SUMMARY
(Erase heading not required.)

Army Form C. 2118

Place	Date	Hour	Summary of Events and Information	Remarks and references to Appendices
In the field	3/7		ADoS IV Corps visited before	
	12/7		Took Major Other Ironside to Mont Lagache.	
	15/7		Inspected water depot & workshop	
	16/7		ADMS called regarding unwatering for Red Barn.	
	17/7		Colonel Nash before & all Trench areas shewn.	
	20/7		Ironside called about lower Trench.	
	25/7		Dec 656 Tank visited & itinerary.	
	28/7		Academy visited hospl	

Lawrason Shiver
Colonel
DADoS 35th Division

Army Form C. 2118

WAR DIARY
or
INTELLIGENCE SUMMARY ADMS 35th Division

(Erase heading not required.)

Instructions regarding War Diaries and Intelligence
Summaries are contained in F.S. Regs., Part II.
and the Staff Manual respectively. Title Pages
will be prepared in manuscript.

WO 95/5

Place	Date	Hour	Summary of Events and Information	Remarks and references to Appendices
	2/5/17		Visits to R.A. reference admin[istration] return of 154" Fd Amb Rations	contd
	3/5/17		Visits ADMS 4 Corps regarding return of winter clothing	contd
	4/5/17		2nd in 10 days DADMS Reserve	contd
	5/5/17		ADMS 61st Division called reference superior S.O. clothing	contd
	6/5/17		Re Amb water report	contd
	7/5/17		Arranged programme for relief of winter clothing after evacuation with ADMS IV Corps	contd
	8/5/17		Visits ADMS IV Corps Res IV Corps Rachel with Ra Amb to arrange for Amb for evacuation gas to casualty st.	contd
	10/5/17		Handed over dumps, area places at Roveres to IV Corps Message O'Brien	contd
	10/5/17		Drs[?] units area with DADMS to collect pur[?] for James depot	contd
	12/5/17		Attd Recl Board of Enquiry re unnecessaries winter clothing	contd

Army Form C. 2118

WAR DIARY
or
INTELLIGENCE SUMMARY
(Erase heading not required.)

Instructions regarding War Diaries and Intelligence Summaries are contained in F.S. Regs., Part II. and the Staff Manual respectively. Title Pages will be prepared in manuscript.

Place	Date	Hour	Summary of Events and Information	Remarks and references to Appendices
	20/5/17		A.D.S. XI Corps called. Moved to new dépôt near Nurlu	Nurlu
	21/5/17		O.C. trucks dépôt a shop.	Lens
	22/5/17		A.D.S. XI Corps called	Lens
	23/5/17		A.D.S. XV and A.D.M.S. called to dumped stores and undercutting to butts.	Lens
	24/5/17		A.D.S. XV Corps called to dumped stores.	Lens
	26/5/17		A.D.S. XV Corps visits dépôt, vehs.	Lens

Guns & Vehicles condemned and replaced during May 1917

O.R. A.2 18 pr. 5 lieutenants Replaced – May 2 in June
M.L. – M 5" Hows.   1   — do —   Not yet replaced
Carriages O.R. 18 pr. 1   — do —   Replaced 6-17
— do — M 5" How   1   — do —   Not yet replaced
Gun Limbers   1   — do —   — do — not replaced
15 pdr. Limbered G.S. Love Bodies   1
Carts Officers Mess   1
Gilkon Travelling thermojets
Lewis G.M.

(A.D.S.S. XV Corps)
(Capt.)

1875 Wt. W593/826 1,000,000 4/15 T.B.C. & A. A.D.S.S./Forms/C. 2118.

● Duplicate ●

WAR DIARY

INTELLIGENCE SUMMARY

Army Form C. 2118

D.A.D.S. 35th Division
May 1917.

(Erase heading not required.)

Instructions regarding War Diaries and Intelligence Summaries are contained in F. S. Regs., Part II. and the Staff Manual respectively. Title Pages will be prepared in manuscript.

Place	Date	Hour	Summary of Events and Information	Remarks and references to Appendices
	2/5/17		Visited R.R.A. reference administration of 154th Fd. Regt.	[illeg]
	3/5/17		Visited ADS 4 Corps regarding return of winter clothing	[illeg]
	6/5/17		Started 10 days sick leave	[illeg]
	8/5/17		DADS 61st Division called reference suspense S10 clothing	[illeg]
			Daily water kept	
	9/5/17		Arranged programme for return of winter clothing after consultation with ADS IV Corps	[illeg]
	10/5/17		Visited ADS IV Corps Res IV Corps Railhead with DADS to arrange for trucks for evacuation of winter clothing	[illeg]
	13/5/17		Handed over dumped area stores at Rosières to IV Corps Salvage Officer	[illeg]
	15/5/17		Visited rest camp with DADS to select site for next depot	[illeg]
	19/5/17		Held Rest Board of Survey on unserviceable winter clothing	[illeg]

WAR DIARY

Army Form C. 2118

D.A.D.O.S. 25th Division
May 1917

INTELLIGENCE SUMMARY

(Erase heading not required.)

Place	Date	Hour	Summary of Events and Information	Remarks and references to Appendices
	20/5/17		ADOS XI Corps called. Moved to new area near Nurlu	Maud
	21/5/17		G.O.C. visits depot & shops.	Lewis
	22/5/17		ADOS XI Corps called.	Lewis
	23/5/17		AA & QMG and ADMS called re dumped stores and undercloths	Lewis
			In both.	
	24/5/17		ADOS XI Corps called re dumped stores.	Lewis
	26/5/17		ADOS XV Corps visits depots & shops.	Lewis
			Guns available condemned and replaced during May 1917	
			Ord QF 18 pr 5. Condemned. Replaced in May 2 in June	
			-do- 4.5 How -do- not yet replaced 1.6.17	
			Carriages QF 18 pr 1 -do- Replaced 1.6.17	
			-do- 4.5 How -do- not yet replaced	
			Guns Lewis -do- and replaced	
			15 gone Lieutenant G.S. Iorn Perkin	
			Leaf Officer wears	(Authorised Wear)
			Military Travelling Complete	Leaf
			Coats & alex	

1875 Wt. W593/826 1,000,000 4/15 J.B.C. & A. A.D.S.S./Forms/C. 2118.

WAR DIARY
or
INTELLIGENCE SUMMARY

Army Form C. 2118

DADDS 35-2

6/16

Place	Date	Hour	Summary of Events and Information	Remarks and references to Appendices
J. said	6/3/17		Attended conference at ADO's Office 3rd Corps	Cans
	6/7/17		Visited G.O.C. 106th Inf Bde & O.C. 15th LFA 9, 19th DG 9 & 17th R Scots	Cans
	6/10/17		Attended weekly conference at Corps HQ & had C, ADDS	Cans
	6/14/17		Visited L.O.O. Boulan reference June	Cans
	6/17/17		Attended ADDS weekly conference at Corps HQ	Cans
	6/18/17		ADDS 3rd Corps visited Depôt	Cans
	6/21/17		Visited Haymaking Party at Col Lecaille 6th Sussex Regt (TF) assumed duties of Salvage Officer vice S/Lt Macdonald Scottish Rifles attached 17th R Scots	Cans
	6/24/17		Attended ADDS weekly conference at Corps HQ	Cans
	6/25/17		Visited G.O.C. 104th and 106th Infy Bdes also 10th Bombs Store with DADMS	Cans

Army Form C. 2118

WAR DIARY
or
INTELLIGENCE SUMMARY

(Erase heading not required.)

Instructions regarding War Diaries and Intelligence Summaries are contained in F.S. Regs., Part II. and the Staff Manual respectively. Title Pages will be prepared in manuscript.

Place	Date	Hour	Summary of Events and Information	Remarks and references to Appendices
	3/7		Attended conference at A.D.S. Office 3rd Centy	
	7/7		Visited H.Q. 102nd Inf. Bde. at O.C. 15th H.L.I., 19th R.S., & 17th R.S.F.,	
	10/7		Attended weekly conference at Corps H.Q. held by A.D.M.S.	
	14/7		Visited R.A.P. bottom of Scherpenberg	
	17/7		Attended ADMS weekly conference at Corps H.Q.	
	18/7		AP of 3rd Centy under heavy [?]	
	21/7		Divisional Sanitary Party at [?] consists [?] duties of Sanitary officer visited R.A.P.s [?] Rifles attached to R. Scots	
	24/7		Attended ADMS weekly conference at Corps H.Q.	
	25/7		Visited H.Q. C. 101st and 102nd Infy Bdes. Also Hd. Bomb store under Scherpenberg	

1875 Wt. W593/826 1,000,000 4/15 T.R.C. & A. A.D.S.S./Forms/C. 2118.

Army Form C. 2118

WAR DIARY
or
INTELLIGENCE SUMMARY
(Erase heading not required.)

Instructions regarding War Diaries and Intelligence Summaries are contained in F. S. Regs., Part II. and the Staff Manual respectively. Title Pages will be prepared in manuscript.

Place	Date	Hour	Summary of Events and Information	Remarks and references to Appendices
In the Field	26/7		Visited Haymaking Party. Mr visited ADOS 3rd Corps regarding use also for the 105th D.S.	(ams)
	27/7		At Sark roles assumed duties of Salvage Officer vice Col Searle Sussex Regt (TF)	(ams) vice
	28/7		Visited OC 35' DAC.	(ams)
			Guns and Vehicles condemned during the month	
			Ord. QF 18pdr — 5 — not yet replaced	
			Carriages QF 15pdr — 1 — do — do	
			Guns Vickers '303' — 1 —	
			Wagons Limbered RE — 1 —	
			Wont Ordnce —	
			Wagons Limbered RE Complete — 1	Replaced
			Carts Watr Mark I — 1	
			Kitchens Travelling — 1	(Anwdson Shorer) Capt
			Wont Jardine	ADOS 35' Division

WAR DIARY
or
INTELLIGENCE SUMMARY

Army Form C. 2118

Place	Date	Hour	Summary of Events and Information	Remarks and references to Appendices
	26/7		Visited Huysinghoff Park. Mr visited N.E. of 2nd Echelon & picking up also 0 for the 105th O.R.S. Rue R.Div.	
	27/7		At Boen Reston to ordinary duties of Salvage Officer vice Col. Clarke Sussex Regt. (T.F.)	
	28/7		Visited a.c. 35th Div.	
			Guns and Vehicles concerned during the month	
				Not yet replaced
			Gun 6" 15pdr 6 -	
			Limber Q.F 15pdr -	
			Gun Vickers · 303 -	10 -- 10
			Wagon Limber R.E. -	
			Home Patten -	
			Wagon Cookers R.E Complete -	} Replaced
			Carts Salt Trench F -	
			Kitchen Travelling :- -	
			Hand Jantia -	Cavalry in Shorn Lye

A.D.S.S. 35th Division

WAR DIARY
or
INTELLIGENCE SUMMARY

Army Form C. 2118

(Erase heading not required.)

Date	Hour	Summary of Events and Information	Remarks and references to Appendices
1/7/17		11 Wagons limbered GS arrived completing Infantry Scale for the carriage of Lewis Guns. During the month of June the following Guns etc were overhauled and repaired in the Regtl Armr's Shop. Guns Lewis. 303 — 200 " Vickers . 303 — 48 " Hotchkiss Rifles MkI — 48 Bicycles — 108 Pistols — 302 Machine Lewis Guns — 170 Pistols — 110 Steel Helmets Vison Slits — 1084 do —do— Removed 1094 Ears but included	
2/7/17		Sent to OC French mission list of French stores salvaged. 500 Rifles & 1800 Drills etherish.	
3/7/17		Visited OC 23rd Manc's Regt regarding clothing for his unit. Inspected men & parade issued for 100 Pistols. SD clothing now being supplied does not appear to be up to Standard of clothing issued in the early days of the war.	
4/7/17		Observed a large abandoned dump of shell cases in the Boulonnese area. Sent lorries to collect same 14,160 shell cases ready for Base, arranged for their removal by Decauville Railway.	
5/7/17		Sent two Tailors from Mt Galon Platz to 16th K.D. for 2 days to assist in carrying out repairs to clothing for a special parade.	

WAR DIARY
or
INTELLIGENCE SUMMARY

Army Form C. 2118

Place	Date	Hour	Summary of Events and Information	Remarks and references to Appendices
	6.7.17		Visited NCS area. Chose site for Salvage depot also for Recuville Railway and through the depot meaning a siding of [?] work. Sent NCO lorries to collect Gas & Iron for Dumps.	Appx 3
	7.7.17		Work Army, Tailors and Shoemakers Shops to NCS area	Appx 4
	8.7.17		Work. Other Units and Offices to NCS area. Built up long standings	Appx 5
	9.7.17		A.A.Q.M.G came with OC Recuville Railway to arrange for special siding to be built which will make all Ordnance Salvage work to be done without using horses	Appx 6
	10.7.17		Visited R.O.O at NCS wanted to arrange for 2 men and 1 NCO to be attached to him to work the Recuville when working	Appx 7
	11.7.17		Held a consultation with "G" & [?] re G.O. reference number of Trench mortars returned & sent some to Base for number returned. Visited GOC 104th Bde and B.G. 17th R.B, 18th R.B & 23rd Manch - Ordnance advises send everyone returned.	Appx 8
	12.7.17		Trench authorities evacuated all cables direct to NCS. 15 GS wagons returned to do the work.	
			A.A.Q.M.G visited Depot. Suggested certain improvements which have been carried out. ADOS 3rd Corps inspected depot.	Appx 9

Army Form C. 2118

WAR DIARY
or
INTELLIGENCE SUMMARY
(Erase heading not required.)

Instructions regarding War Diaries and Intelligence Summaries are contained in F.S. Regs., Part II. and the Staff Manual respectively. Title Pages will be prepared in manuscript.

Place	Date	Hour	Summary of Events and Information	Remarks and references to Appendices
	13.7.17		Visited R&OS Army Head Qrs	
	14.7.17		Attended conference at office of A.D.O.S. 3rd Corps.	
	15.7.17		Observed a large quantity of wire, pickets & photos exhibit returning from Army H.Q. Sent two lorries to collect.	
	17.7.17		Visited M.G. section of D.O.C. also a/c rep. of the 18th H.C.9 & 17th R.Sets. Visited A.D.O.S. 3rd Corps reference the armouring of Guns & gun parts from Army Gun Park.	
	18.7.17		Saw a German Trench Mortar and handed it over to "G" for information & inspection.	
	19.7.17		Visited 1st & 10th Trains re the salving of ratine. Arranged to serve at my HQrs and the Train will bomb them periodically. Two Lewis Guns received for mechanical Inspection. Sent 6 men with 1 N.C.O. 1 Tent & 6 days rations to Colony Valley for salvage work. Sent the 16 Vickers Guns of 241st (Ment) M/Co Gun Co & in for inspection and regulation	
	20.7.17			

WAR DIARY
or
INTELLIGENCE SUMMARY
(Erase heading not required.)

Army Form C. 2118

Instructions regarding War Diaries and Intelligence Summaries are contained in F. S. Regs., Part II. and the Staff Manual respectively. Title Pages will be prepared in manuscript.

Place	Date	Hour	Summary of Events and Information	Remarks and references to Appendices
At the Base	31.7.17		Went on Haymaking Party with the AD of Supply an Ordnance point of view also paws SE 105" Bde and all CO.s of Vdiv. No Ordnance complaints. Nothing learned from CO.s	(initials)
	20.7.17		attended conference held by ADOS 3rd Corps	(initials)
			Visited HQ 106" Bde and OC 15th NAS	(initials)
	24.7.17		Visited Railhead Road with DaDug regarding the 60 c.m. railway. 25.7.17 It was decided that loses must be used for a further pilot period regarding Ordnance matters	(initials)
			Visited GOC 104" Bde and L.O. 18" LT regarding Ordnance matters	(initials)
	26.7.17		Saw Dom 3rd Corps reference 5 GS Wagons of 106" Bde. These will be repaired 2 for dim starting tomorrow	(initials)
	27.7.17		Observed large abandoned dumps at Luggata. D "Q" men placed be sent from salvage to collect. Agreed upon 6 men, 15 C.O. Sent about 6 days rations leave lorries. Timber won't be will be handed over to the RE dumps at St Emilee	(initials)
	31.7.17		Principal items of work done in Workshops during July:	(initials)
			Limbers mechanical repaired 67
			" Wheelers do do 17
			Bicycles do do 148
			Rifles do do 346
			Saws do do 25
			Steel Helmets do do 217
			Magazines Lewis Gun do do 287

Chas Hanson
Da DOS 35" Division

1875 Wt. W593/826 1,000,000 4/15 J.B.C. & A. A.D.S.S./Forms/C. 2118.

WAR DIARY or **INTELLIGENCE SUMMARY**

Army Form C. 2118

(Erase heading not required.)

DADS 357

July 1918

Place	Date	Hour	Summary of Events and Information	Remarks and references to Appendices
	1.8.17		Visited ADOS 3rd Corps re list of returns, also called on DS 3rd Corps. 2 German M/G Guns captured by 25th Division. Commenced to use the Acheville Railway	AW?
	2.8.17		Returned 3 lorries to Supply Col. retained one for special work	AW?
	3.8.17		Visited Rudland regarding delay in despatch of trucks by Beaurell. Found and salved a large water tank	AW?
	4.8.17		DDOS 3rd Army visited the 2 German machine Guns captured by 25th Division. Despatched to Base the 2 German machine Guns captured by 25th Division	AW? AW?
	5.8.17		Visited DDOS 3rd Army, also called at Army Gun Park for Gun spares urgently required	AW?
	6.8.17		Despatched to Base German Trench Mortar No 1083 Patd by me on 15/7/17	AW?
	8.8.17		Visited ADOS 3rd Corps re extra lorries required for Special Purposes, also called on DDS 3rd Corps Troops for same reason	AW?

1875 Wt. W593/826 1,000,000 4/15 J.B.C. & A. A.D.S.S./Forms/C. 2118.

WAR DIARY or INTELLIGENCE SUMMARY

Army Form C. 2118

(Erase heading not required.)

Instructions regarding War Diaries and Intelligence Summaries are contained in F.S. Regs., Part II. and the Staff Manual respectively. Title Pages will be prepared in manuscript.

Place	Date	Hour	Summary of Events and Information	Remarks and references to Appendices
	9.8.17		Visited Gun Park and Div. Stores. Staff Capt. W. Laws Dismounted Brigade called re Divl. matters. Arrange to meet A.A. meeting at Kruisstraat lines.	Laws
	10.8.17		D.A.D.O.S. W.L. Law son called reference receipt for No 3 Bde of 11" & 12" rifle Gun Squads. Attended conference at office of A.D.O.S.	Laws
	12.8.17		Visited 10" Bde H.Q. re Special Stores. Reports made to "A" Bty. re solo obtained necessary authority for same	Laws
	13.8.17		Special rifle Gun Mounting received for trial and experts. Issued to Bn H.Q.	Laws
	14.8.17		Visited Gun Park and obtained Special Stores for Bn H.Q. D.A.D.O.S. HQ. re	Laws
	15.8.17		Called re coaching appearances	Laws
	17.8.17		Visited G.O.C. 10" & 100" Iny. Bdes	
	18.8.17		57 Vickers Bands. To Kruigle Crops and 45 Bells ammn urgently sent for from Army Park in reference to demand from Bn H.Q. Attended conference held by A.D.O.S. 3rd Corps. 2 Vickers Gun Remounted reach for 105" M.G Coy & 13" M.G Squadron.	Laws
	20.8.17		74 Magazine Lewis Gun Sent up to 105" Bde. & Sent car to Army Gun Park for 200 Magazine Lewis Gun & 100 Belts ammn which were urgently received.	Laws

Army Form C. 2118

WAR DIARY
or
INTELLIGENCE SUMMARY
(Erase heading not required.)

Instructions regarding War Diaries and Intelligence Summaries are contained in F.S. Regs., Part II. and the Staff Manual respectively. Title Pages will be prepared in manuscript.

Place	Date	Hour	Summary of Events and Information	Remarks and references to Appendices
	20.8.17		2. 2" Stokes Mortars 106" T.M.B. destroyed. Replacements sent for. 105" M/c Gun C/s & 12" M/c Gun Sand each issued with new Vickers Gun	[and?]
	21.8.17		A.D.O.S. 3rd Corps called re the 51 Barrel Vickers Gun demanded. Ordered the 51 M/s Barrel to be sent to Corps M.O. for transmission to the army. 1 3" Stokes Mortar 105" T.M.B. destroyed	[and?]
	22.6.17		Unserviceable Vickers Gun from 12th M/c Gun Sqd destroyed to base	[and?]
	22.8.17		1 Lewis Gun 19th D.I. & 15th H.L.I. destroyed. Replacements demanded.	[and?]
	23.8.17		Issued 19th D.G. 9 & 18th H.L.I. 3 each with new Lewis Gun	[and?]
	24.8.17		2 Lewis Guns 15th N.F.& Derbys destroyed. Sent for replacement. Repaired in 10th Army Shop the damaged Vickers Gun of 105" M/cc Gun C/s. Returned also to unit and withdrew new gun which was issued on 20". One A.A 15th & 80 B.M.G.S. of D/157 Bde R.F.A. condemned for firing	
	25.8.17		Issued 106" T.M.B. with 7 new 3 inch Stokes Mortar. 106" M/cc Gun C/s reported Vickers Gun out of action. Ordered the gun into Army Shop for repair. 1 M.K.IV Tripod Mounting issued to 106" M/cc Gun C/s to replace one destroyed. 5 3" Stokes Mortars belonging to 106" T.M.B. destroyed. Demanded new mortars by wire	[and?]

1875 Wt. W593/826 1,000,000 4/15 J.R.C. & A. A.D.S.S./Forms/C. 2118.

WAR DIARY or INTELLIGENCE SUMMARY

Army Form C. 2118

Place	Date	Hour	Summary of Events and Information	Remarks and references to Appendices
	26.8.17		16 Lewis Guns asked for both 105ᵗ and 106ᵗ w/co Lewis Guns DP.O.S 3rd army and D.D.O.S 3rd army office inspected Lewis, Workshops and were expected into the question of outrages and immediate issue. D.D.O.S 3rd army also demanded the issue of 57 Lewis Barrels and S.M. ayon boxes these Barrels and repaired all 6 Lewis Barrels and were issued immediate	Cant.O
	27.8.17		15ᵗ A.R.S demanded 5 Lewis Guns 63 spare parts bags, 120 magazines to replace other damages issued for replacements returned to A.O.S 3rd Corps the unserviceable Vickers Gun Barrels which were returned by army demanded for 19ᵗ D.R.S. 1 Lewis Gun & 2 spare parts bags to replace losses by shell fire. 2 Lewis tents blown down by gale.	Cant.O
	28.8.17		Issued 19ᵗ D.R.S with new Lewis Gun & 2 spare part bags.	Cant.O
In the Field	29.8.17		Remanded 2 Lewis Guns for 15ᵗ Lancers. Issued from shop which was received & repaired.	Cant.O
	30.6.17			Cant.O
	31.8.17		Old Q.Z. 15ᵗ⁄15ᵗ N°. 2694 on charge of 12/157ᵗ D.R. R.F.A condemned for severe neck jacket demanded	Cant.O

Army Form C. 2118

WAR DIARY
or
INTELLIGENCE SUMMARY
(Erase heading not required.)

Instructions regarding War Diaries and Intelligence Summaries are contained in F. S. Regs., Part II. and the Staff Manual respectively. Title Pages will be prepared in manuscript.

Place	Date	Hour	Summary of Events and Information	Remarks and references to Appendices
			Principal items of work done in Work Shops during August 1917	
Shop			Work Performed	
Armourer		Average number of men employed daily		
		11	Vickers Guns overhauled & repaired — 25	
			Lewis —do— —do— —do— — 111	
			Magazines Lewis Guns —do— — 1106	
			Tripod Mountings Vickers Gun Repaired — 5	
			Rifles overhauled & repaired — 839	
			Pistols —do— —do— — 35	
			Steel Helmets —do— —do— — 81	
			Bayonets —do— —do— — 51	
			Bicycles —do— —do— — 73	Sgd.
			Rifles cleaned & sent to Base — 567	
Shoemakers		4	Boots Soles & heels renewed — 252	
			—do— overhauled, paired & despatched to Base — 1050	
			Manufacture of 100 Rifle Buckets for Grenade rifles	Cont.

1875. Wt. W593/826 1,000,000 4/15 T.B.C. & A. A.D.S.S./Forms/C. 2118.

Army Form C. 2118

WAR DIARY
or
INTELLIGENCE SUMMARY
(Erase heading not required.)

Instructions regarding War Diaries and Intelligence Summaries are contained in F.S. Regs., Part II. and the Staff Manual respectively. Title Pages will be prepared in manuscript.

Place	Date	Hour	Summary of Events and Information			Remarks and references to Appendices
			Average number of men employed daily	Work Performed		
Shop				Outside JO Orchard, clenches & repairs	720	Cwt
				Other Garments — 20 — 10 —	60	
Gailes			3			

31/8/17

Ainslie Sproer
Captain
R.A.O.C. 35th Division

1875 Wt. W593/826 1,000,000 4/15 T.R.C. & A. A.D.S.S./Forms/C. 2118.

WAR DIARY or INTELLIGENCE SUMMARY

Army Form C. 2118

DADOS 352

Vol 19

Place	Date	Hour	Summary of Events and Information	Remarks and references to Appendices
In the Field	1.7.17		Ord. O. S. 15 for N° 1875 on charge of 15/151st Bde RFA conference for "Scarpe" fire. Replacements demanded.	
			— Same Series Modus on charge of 105' T.M.B. destroyed by hostile fire. Replacements demanded.	
	2.7.17		2 Vickers Guns on charge of 241st M/Co Gun Coy destroyed by shell fire. Replacements demanded.	
	3.7.17		1st S. Staff Yorks repulse 7 Lewis Guns required. Defence also 9 empties Opno foot bags issued for replacements captured.	
	4.7.17		Issued 241st M/Co Gun with 2 Vickers Guns 117'2/5 Yorks with 7 Lewis Guns & 9 Spare Part Bags. A.D.O.S. 7 Inspected depot estafo	
	5.7.17		Visited S.C. 106' Bde & O.C. 15th MRS. 19' R & S. 117' S Yorks on Ordnance matters. A.D.O.S 3rd Army called with A.D.O.S N°3 Corps to inspect depot & to enquire into system of Ordnance issues in the Field etc.	
	6.7.17		A.Ds Ord. G with Dad Vg visited depot. Visited 30 reference new pattern water carrier. Visited Rucken re complaints about boots.	

WAR DIARY
or
INTELLIGENCE SUMMARY

(Erase heading not required.)

Army Form C. 2118

Instructions regarding War Diaries and Intelligence Summaries are contained in F.S. Regs., Part II. and the Staff Manual respectively. Title Pages will be prepared in manuscript.

Place	Date	Hour	Summary of Events and Information	Remarks and references to Appendices
In the Field	6.9.17		Sent in with Salvage Stores Visited DADOS HQrs Divison re Magazine for Lewis Gun and brought them away	Contd
	7.9.17		Visited 3rd Army Gun Park for urgent Gun Stores also called upon ADOS 3rd Army	Contd
	8.9.17		Visited G.O.C. 104th Bde & OC 20th Lancs Fusrs re conference about Snipers	Contd
	9.9.17		Attended conference at Corps HQ & recd 21 ADOS	Contd
	10.9.17		Visited DDOS 3rd Army & called at Gun Park for stores	Contd
	12.9.17		Inspected Clothing & Leather of D.A.C. called upon Don re Portion Wagon for such LofC also called upon ADOS 3rd Corps re personnel	Contd
	13.9.17		ADOS 3rd Corps inspected Repair Workshop	Contd
	14.9.17		Visited ADOS 3rd Corps re handing over of defects etc etc	Contd

WAR DIARY
or
INTELLIGENCE SUMMARY

(Erase heading not required.)

Army Form C. 2118

Instructions regarding War Diaries and Intelligence Summaries are contained in F. S. Regs., Part II. and the Staff Manual respectively. Title Pages will be prepared in manuscript.

Place	Date	Hour	Summary of Events and Information	Remarks and references to Appendices
	16.9.17		Granted leave from 26th Sept. Lieut Black attended conference at office of A.D.O.S.	Lieut ?
	22.9.17		R.A.O.S. Bn. Conf. inspected depot	Lieut ?
	23.9.17		Lieut Black attended conference at Corps about Div Advanced Workshops. Wrote out A.O.S. 105" T.M.B. upaired 3-inch Stokes Mortars destroyed by hostile fire. Replacement demanded by wire.	Lieut ?
	27.9.17		3-inch Stokes Mortars issued to 105" T.M. Battery.	Lieut ?
	28.9.17		Visited new area. to select site for depot workshops. Visited A.D.O.S 3rd Corps also to work out arr¹s to arrange admin¹ of R.A. units	Lieut ?
	30.9.17		attended conference at Corps & held by the A.D.O.S. List of principal items of work done in Divisional Workshop during Sept¹	Lieut ?
			Tailors Shop 400 pairs Puttees cleaned & repaired in addition Armourers repairs to Jackets Trousers Pants etc etc.	Lieut ?

WAR DIARY
or
INTELLIGENCE SUMMARY
(Erase heading not required.)

Army Form C. 2118

Place	Date	Hour	Summary of Events and Information	Remarks and references to Appendices
Armourers Shop			225 pairs Boots Soles & heels — 43	Inst.
			94 " " " " — 20	
			2028 " Soles, Pairs despatched to Base — 790	
			Armourers Shop	
			Lewis Guns cleaned, overhauled & repaired — 130	
			Vickers do do — 169	
			Magazine Lewis Guns do do — 11	
			Bicycles do do — 3	
			Steel Helmets do do — 25	
			Pistols do do — 114	
			Gun Scan do do — 96	
			Rifles do do — 13	
			Bayonets Scabbards do do —	
			Washing Tripod do do —	Inst.

30/9/17

L. A. Walton Plover
DADOS 35th Division

Ruth Field

War Diary.
D.A.D. Ordce 35 Divn.

Period – Feby. 1-28th 1918

Volume No 2.

Original

WAR DIARY

A.D.S. 35 Division   Army Form C. 2118

INTELLIGENCE SUMMARY

October 1917.

Vol 20

Place	Date	Hour	Summary of Events and Information	Remarks and references to Appendices
	1-10-17		Moved stores and photo to new area to A.D.o.S. Hd Qrs.	Capt?
	2.10.17		Were office and stays to new area. Reported arrival	Capt?
	3.10.17		Visited ADoS 17th Corps. also Corps Salvage Stores. Visited new works	Capt?
			Park to ascertain requirements of Camp Equipment etc.	
	4.10.17		Visited S.C. 104th & 105th B.d.s to arrange Ordnance refilling points in their Divisional	Capt?
			areas and obtained from ADoS 17th Corps all reserve camp equipment for	
			Reported Batt.ns	
	5.10.17		Visited H.Q. 106th Bdd on general Ordnance matters. Drafted Mobile Vety Secto in	Capt?
			arrange to horse float and arranged with S.M. for immediate repair	
	6.10.17		Concluded Vickers Guns of 104th M/cc Gun Co. DAQMG watch refl	Capt?
			Drafted Ordnance refilling points of 104th & 105th Bdes Visits Army Gun	
			Park to draw urgent gun spares	
			Visited S.O.C 104th & 105th Bdes, also G.O.C of Balln in these Bdes & L.G. 106th	Capt?
	7-10-17		Orders received to prepare to move northward. Arranged with R.T.O for the	Capt?
	8.10.17		allotment of tr trucks for conveyance of stores. Also Visited S.C. 106th	Capt?
			& machine gun indent	
	9.10.17		Visited Gun Park for Gun Stores. Transport arrived from Sonchez to	Capt?
			Northern Base and suspended issues until completion of move	

WAR DIARY
or
INTELLIGENCE SUMMARY

(Erase heading not required.)

Army Form C. 2118

Place	Date	Hour	Summary of Events and Information	Remarks and references to Appendices
	10.10.17		Visited neb area to select site for repot and shops	Cont
	12.10.17		Moved office & lines salvage section to arncke. Reported arrival to D.A.Q.	Cont
	13.10.17		Sent 1 N.C.O. & Salvage party to check places for repot park, no look being available.	Cont
	14.10.17		Inder Reed area to select depot.	Cont
	15.10.17		A. a D.M.S. called. Sent advance party to new area. Visited depot. Battn Hangar of club. Completed the erection of 4 shelters 30'x30'.	Cont
	16.10.17		Visited Bn H.Q. in Proven area. Sent lorries to Calais for 6000 bundles Salvation.	Cont
	17.10.17		MMMMMM Moved Stores, offices & plant to Elverdinghe	Cont
	18.10.17		21,000 sand bags arrived. Sollen arrived. also 6000 bundles Salvation.	Cont
	19.10.17		Lewis 3000 Waterproof Sur Sheeter Salvation received. Special reserve of 10 Lewis Gun fir reserve received.	Cont
	20.10.17		Officer advanced announced at Boesinghe to control the immediate issue of Lewis Gun Magnet to relieve casualties also effect argent repairs. Also established an advance Salvage Section at Boesinghe	Cont

Army Form C. 2118

WAR DIARY
or
INTELLIGENCE SUMMARY
(Erase heading not required.)

Instructions regarding War Diaries and Intelligence Summaries are contained in F.S. Regs., Part II. and the Staff Manual respectively. Title Pages will be prepared in manuscript.

Place	Date	Hour	Summary of Events and Information	Remarks and references to Appendices
In the Field	21/7		1 Vickers & 1 Lewis Gun destroyed by Shell fire	Appx I
	22/7		Replaced Vickers & Lewis Guns recovered on 20th	Appx II
	23/7		3 Vickers Guns damaged by shell fire & destroyed	
			4 S. Gun Carriage damaged by D/154 Bde RGA by place also locally	Appx III
			destroyed. Issued 3 Vickers Gun to replace losses & 2 gun	
	24/7		1 Vickers gun carriage damaged & replaced 1 destroyed by shell fire	
	25/7		Following Guns &c demanded to replace losses & shell fire.	Appx IV
			Guns Vickers - 1	
			" Lewis 6.	
			Car Q.J 15 pdr - 1	
			" H.5 How. - 1	
			Carriages Q.J 4.5 How. 2	
			Wagons Limbered BS - 1	
			" Stores J 2	
			" Rations J 2	
			Wagons Am - Q.J 15 pdr J - 1	
			Shackles	
			Barrels 3" and plates J - 7	
			Wheels	
			A.A. O. in G. 35th Division visited depot	

Army Form C. 2118

WAR DIARY
or
INTELLIGENCE SUMMARY
(Erase heading not required.)

Instructions regarding War Diaries and Intelligence Summaries are contained in F. S. Regs, Part II. and the Staff Manual respectively. Title Pages will be prepared in manuscript.

Place	Date	Hour	Summary of Events and Information	Remarks and references to Appendices
In the Field	26/10/17		Following Guns &c demand to replace casualties & also allotment of Guns issued 188 Prisma hay demand Remanded	Cont
			Received	
			Wagns am Q 215 par — 5	
			Guns Lewis .303 — 16 — 16	
			" Vickers .303 — 6 — 1	
			Barrels 3" Stokes Mortar — 1 — 7	
	27/10/17		Guns Lewis .303 — 22 — 17	
			" Vickers .303" — 2 — 7	
			Wagns am aKinds Q7 15par — — 1	Cont
	28/10/17		Docs 5' Army verbal dept of chapr	
			Following Guns demanded & received during the day	
			Ock Q7 15ph a Garrage — 1 — Blown on Enemy artillery	
			Guns Vickers .303 — 1 — 2	
			Wagns Am Q 7 15par — 1 — 5	
			Guns Lewis .303 — — 11	Cont
	29/10/17		Synder Q 7 15par Wagns Am — 5 — 1	
			Guns Vickers .303 — — 1	Cont

Army Form C. 2118

WAR DIARY
or
INTELLIGENCE SUMMARY
(Erase heading not required.)

Instructions regarding War Diaries and Intelligence Summaries are contained in F. S. Regs., Part II. and the Staff Manual respectively. Title Pages will be prepared in manuscript.

Place	Date	Hour	Summary of Events and Information	Remarks and references to Appendices
	30/9		1 Lewis Gun returned to reference 1 [illegible]	[illegible]
	31/9		Lewis Gun received to replace casualty of 30th. 15[pr] Q.F Gun in charge of 6/15A instead of 8 Som. Yr. Carriages. Statement showing casualties and replacements of Guns Carriages during the month.	[illegible]

Guns.

	Demands	Received	Remarks
Ord Q.F. 18 pdr	23	15	13 all used 1 still aws
do H.S. How.	1	1	
Carriage Q.F. 18 pdr	1	3	1(?)11 still aws
do H.S. How	6	6	
Wagon Am Q.F. 15 pdr with Limbers	14	14	
Guns Lewis .303	14	14	
" Vickers .303	7	7	
" Barrels 3" Stokes Mortar	3	3	1 Out
Sents officers Mess (Sale tent)	2	2	2 —do—
Wagons Limbered G.S.	3	3	1 —no—
" " " R.E.	3	3	2 —do—
" G S M.T.	5	5[?]	5 —do—
" Pontoon R.E.	2	2	

WAR DIARY or INTELLIGENCE SUMMARY

Army Form C. 2118

(Erase heading not required.)

Instructions regarding War Diaries and Intelligence Summaries are contained in F.S. Regs., Part II. and the Staff Manual respectively. Title Pages will be prepared in manuscript.

Place	Date	Hour	Summary of Events and Information	Remarks and references to Appendices
			Statement shewing principal items of work during the month of October. See Annex to War Diary	
			Bootmakers Shop	
			Boots repaired — pairs 371	
			Minor repairs — " 213	
			Sundry oddments " 1411	
			— Langer for Base	
			Tailors Shop	
			Puttees overhauled — pairs 945	
			" " Brethus — do 107	
			Other garments: patches, buttons etc 13	
			Garments packed & conditioned for Base 1500	
			Armourers Shop	
			Guns Lewis overhauled — repaired 64	
			" " Brethus — do 29	
			Mounting Tripods — do 13	
			Rifles — do 276	
			Bayonets — do 57	
			Bicycles — do 74	
			Pistols — do 8	
			Magazines Lewis Guns — do 711	
			3/10/17	
			L. Anwatrie Mayor Lieut	
			ADOS 35 Division	

Army Form C. 2118.

WAR DIARY
of
INTELLIGENCE SUMMARY.
(Erase heading not required.)

Instructions regarding War Diaries and Intelligence Summaries are contained in F. S. Regs., Part II. and the Staff Manual respectively. Title pages will be prepared in manuscript.

Place	Date	Hour	Summary of Events and Information	Remarks and references to Appendices
In the Field	1/9/17		Detailed by DADSS Army to attend Course of Instruction in Anmt 20,29,14 Sept	Lieut P
	2/9/17		1 Vickers Gun 165" M.G.Co destroyed by hostile fire 1 horse " 17" W kills " do	Lieut P
	3/9/17		Received instructions to prepare to vacate Refso. Visited new area & collect news of post 1 Lewis & 1 Vickers gun received to replace casualties of the 1st inst	Lieut P
	4/9/17		Outpost of area chosen to be looked over & moved Refso to new area 1 Vickers Gun 241st M/Co condemned for damage by hostile fire 1 Vickers Gun issued to 241st M/Co Gun Co'	Lieut P
	5/9/17		Move office & Cockburn Platss to new area	Lieut P
	6/9/17		6 you G.S blankets received from Base in full issued of 3rd December	Lieut P
	17/9/17		Moved to new area	Lieut P
	18/9/17		Remarked 2 W.S.dros confiscated for 6/15A'BDE to replace 2 totally destroyed by direct ab.	Lieut P
	19/9/17		1 GS (5A"/15A"BDE) condemned for "leaving" Replacement demanded 1 GS (8A"Garage (A/15A"BDE) destroyed by hostile fire do do	Lieut P
	20			

WAR DIARY
or
INTELLIGENCE SUMMARY.

Army Form C. 2118.

(Erase heading not required.)

Place	Date	Hour	Summary of Events and Information	Remarks and references to Appendices
	20/7		DADQMG 35th Div. visited and inspected Depot & Shops. Arrival Train with Corps re road in Depot for transport. 1 QF 18pr (S/157) destroyed to base June. Replacement demanded.	Louis B
	22/7		1 Lewis Gun (14th DLS) destroyed to base June —do— / 1 QF 18pr Carriage (S/157) 18th Dragoons destroyed to base June —do—	Louis B
	23/7		1 Lewis Gun issued to 14th DLS. GOC 35th Division inspected Depot Shops. Presented Military Medal to A/Sgt Kellett (Salvage Coy attached) Inspected Det in quarters.	Louis B
	25/7		Visited HQ of 104th M.Gun Coy.	Louis B
	27/7		Visited ADOS 2nd Corps re Salvage of Gun Stores discussed accuracy of census of Gun Carriages attached to be issued to the QMG.	Louis B
	28/7		AAQMG 35th Div. visited Depot. Also ADOS 2nd & 19th Corps re census of Guns etc.	Louis B
	30/7		2 Lewis Guns (15th Cheshires) at Nieuport Sur. 106" M/Co G/S destroyed by shell fire. Replacements demanded. Dressed by H.Q. Corps. ADOS 2nd Corps called.	Louis B

Army Form C. 2118.

WAR DIARY
or
INTELLIGENCE SUMMARY.
(Erase heading not required.)

Instructions regarding War Diaries and Intelligence Summaries are contained in F. S. Regs., Part II. and the Staff Manual respectively. Title pages will be prepared in manuscript.

Place	Date	Hour	Summary of Events and Information	Remarks and references to Appendices
			Summary of principal items of work performed in Ord. Shops Nov.	
Armt. Shop			Lewis Guns Ordnance Inspection. 107	
			Vickers do do 31	
			Magazine Lewis Gun Repaired 53	
			Mounting Tripod IV do 8	
			Rifles Examined & Repaired 347	
			Steel Helmets do do 22	
			Bayonets & Scabbards do do 61	
			Bicycles do do 74	
			Pistols do do 18	
			Binocular Prism do do 8	
			Prismatic Sirio do do 7	Unset.
			Elastic Torches do do 6	
			Rifles Cleaned, examined & sent to Base 305	
Shoemakers Shop			Boots Repaired, dressed & sent to Ordnance, passed & sent to Base 784	
			" Ordnance passed & sent to Base 2139	
Tailors Shop			Jackets Ordnance sent to Base 3045	
			Trousers do do 2649	
			Putties do do 389	
			" do repaired, passed & sent to Base 1064	

10/13/17

Lauzelsen Major
Da ADS 35 on Corps

Army Form C. 2118.

D.A.D.O.S. 35th Division WAR DIARY

December 1917.

INTELLIGENCE SUMMARY.
(Erase heading not required.)

Instructions regarding War Diaries and Intelligence Summaries are contained in F. S. Regs., Part II. and the Staff Manual respectively. Title pages will be prepared in manuscript.

Place	Date	Hour	Summary of Events and Information	Remarks and references to Appendices
In the Field	Decr 1917			
Southwick	1.12		New Road at Depot started. 3 wagons ammn Q.F 18 pr belonging to 35th D.A.C. destroyed by shell fire.	U
	2.12		Visited 6.00 Calais Base re Indents and Stores generally.	U
	3.12		Returned from visit to 6.00 Calais Base. New W.O. applied for, vice Major Wade. 104 Inf Bde, evacuated to England sick.	U
	6.12		2 Lewis Guns belonging to 4th N. Stafford Regt destroyed by shell fire.	U
	6.12		1 Vickers gun with tripod, 2 H.G.Coy destroyed by shell fire. D.A.D.M.S called re lighting of billets for troops.	U
	9.12		Started moving to Depot at Rouen.	U
	11.12		D.A.R.M.S visited new Depot.	U
	14.12		Const of Engy nry at H.Q. 9pr 19 R Fus on the loss of a limber on charge of 205 Fd Coy R.E. 1-18 pr Gun, A/157 Bde R.F.A destroyed by enemy shell fire.	U
	15.12		L.S.O.1 called at Depot. 2-18 pr Guns A/157 Bde R.F.A condemned through wearing	U

Army Form C. 2118.

A.A.D.O.S. 35th Division WAR DIARY December 1917.
or
INTELLIGENCE SUMMARY.
(Erase heading not required.)

Instructions regarding War Diaries and Intelligence Summaries are contained in F.S. Regs., Part II. and the Staff Manual respectively. Title pages will be prepared in manuscript.

Place	Date	Hour	Summary of Events and Information	Remarks and references to Appendices
In the Field	Decr 1917			
	17th		D.S.O.1 called at Depot re Badges for R.A.	U
	18th		Visited CRA. re Ordnance matters generally and badges for the R.A.	U
	19th		One 18 pr Gun for A/157 Bde R.F.A. received.	U
	20th		Two 18 pr Guns for A/157 Bde R.F.A. received. Three 18 pr Guns belonging to same that condemned - leaving.	U
	25th		Three 18 pr Guns received for A/157 Bde R.F.A.	U
	29th		One 18 pr Gun for C/157 Bde R.F.A. condemned - leaving.	U

Reas Nure Capt
A.A.D.O.S. 35th Division

WAR DIARY.

D.A.D.O.S.

35th Divn.

PERIOD :- 1st. To. 31st January. 1918.

VOLUME. No. 2.

WAR DIARY or INTELLIGENCE SUMMARY

Army Form C. 2118

(Erase heading not required.)

Instructions regarding War Diaries and Intelligence Summaries are contained in F. S. Regs., Part II. and the Staff Manual respectively. Title Pages will be prepared in manuscript.

Place	Date	Hour	Summary of Events and Information	Remarks and references to Appendices
In the Field	5/5		Issued 6/157" Bde R.J.A. with Q.J 15/cr Gun Surface me destroyer	V.S.
	6/5		by hostile fire	V.S.
			Visited D.A.D.O.S. 56th Divn. to arrange taking over of depot & new area	
	7/5		Moved stores to new area	V.S.
	8/5		Took balance of personnel & stores to new area	V.S.
	10/5		R.A.C. & Adj 35" Divn visited depot	V.S.
	12/5		15/cr Gun No 1610 on charge of 6/157" Bde R.J.A. condemned by D.O.O.	V.S.
			A.D.O.S. 2nd Corps visited depot for scrap	
	13/5		D.A.D.v.S. 35" Divn and A.D.O.S. 2nd Corps called	V.S.
	15/5		A.A. & Q.M.G. 35" Divn inspected depot & workshops	V.S.
	18/5		Visited Staff Captain 106" & 121 R.D.L.G.	V.S.
	20/5		3 Q.J. 15/cr Guns condemned by D.O.O. for "Relining"	V.S.
	22/5		Visited Salvage Dump at Blaringhem for stores	V.S.

WAR DIARY
or
INTELLIGENCE SUMMARY

Army Form C. 2118

(Erase heading not required.)

Place	Date	Hour	Summary of Events and Information	Remarks and references to Appendices
Jutland etc	23/8		Q.7 15pr No 4744 on charge of D/157 1Div RGA condemned by Jan. Inspn Ineman in rear of plant level.	U
	24/8		Visited Corps Salvage dump at Vlamertinghe for class myself re. unused damages for cases.	U
	26/8		1 Lewis Gun on charge of 16" Howitzers authgn to repl. p/ed gun. Replacement demanded	U
	27/8		1 Lewis Gun issued to 16" Howitzer	U
	28/8		A.R.O.S. 2nd Corps called re salvage dumps	U
	29/8		Visited RA Salvage Section	U
	30/8		Visited Corps Salvage Dumps at Vlamertinghe for samples	
	31/8		Q.7 15pr No 46117 on charge of G/159 15Div RGA condemned by Jan. Gun damage done by hostile fire, replacement demanded	U

1875 Wt. W593/826 1,000,000 4/15 J.B.C. & A. A.D.S.S./Forms/C. 2118.

WAR DIARY
or
INTELLIGENCE SUMMARY
(Erase heading not required.)

Army Form C. 2118

Place	Date	Hour	Summary of Events and Information	Remarks and references to Appendices
			Statement showing principal items of work performed in our Shops during January 1918	
			Ammunition Shop	
			Lewis Guns overhauled and fixed 24	
			Bicycles do do 106	
			Rifles do do 162	
			Bayonets do do 47	
			Steel Helmets do do 123	
			Binoculars Blumenthal do do 4	
			Coils of remesh rem rifles do do 121	
			Magazine Strin Glm do do 167	
			Watches do do 7	
			Shoemakers Shop	
			Boots repaired from 369	
			" overhauled & sent to Base 833	
			Tailors Shop	
			Suits repaired overseas for 360	
			Garments do do 65	
			do sorted & sent to Base 2490	

Austin Plover
D.A.D.O.S. 35th Division

Army Form C. 2118.

WAR DIARY
or
INTELLIGENCE SUMMARY.

(Erase heading not required.)

Instructions regarding War Diaries and Intelligence Summaries are contained in F. S. Regs., Part II. and the Staff Manual respectively. Title pages will be prepared in manuscript.

Place	Date	Hour	Summary of Events and Information	Remarks and references to Appendices
	1.2.18		Arranged details for reception of rifles & ranges of 4 Infy Batt'ns on reorganization of Infy Bdes	Cont'd
	2.2.18		4 O.B 18pr Guns issued to Batteries to replace casualties etc in Action	Cont'd
			Visited Bde B. re reorganization of Infantry Bde.	Cont'd
	3.2.18 & 6		Receiving not Ranges of Bde 4 Reheaded Infantry Batt'n	Cont'd
	6.2.18		1 Lewis Gun 15 Coolers Lost. 1 O.B 18pr Gun (B/159th Bde Bde) condemned by IOM for damages by shell fire	Cont'd
	7.2.18		Issued 15 Coolers to replace Lewis Gun	Cont'd
	8.2.18		1 Lewis Gun 10th R.B.9 destroyed by shell fire.	Cont'd
	9.2.18		Issued 19th R.B.9 with 1 Lewis Gun	Cont'd
	10.2.18		Attended Court of Inquiry on deficiencies of 23rd Manc Regt	
	11.2.18		Visited DivI Salvage Section	Cont'd

WAR DIARY
or
INTELLIGENCE SUMMARY.

(Erase heading not required.)

Army Form C. 2118.

Instructions regarding War Diaries and Intelligence Summaries are contained in F. S. Regs., Part II. and the Staff Manual respectively. Title pages will be prepared in manuscript.

Place	Date	Hour	Summary of Events and Information	Remarks and references to Appendices
	11.2.18		1 O.R. 15pr Gun returned to B/159 RBd to replace casualty of 7 inst. 1 Vickers Gun 106th MkR Gun BS destroyed by shell fire.	Cont'd
	12.2.18		1 OR 15pr Gun cleaning on charge of B/159 BAC RBd condemned by I.O.M. for damage by shell fire.	Cont'd
	13.2.18		Completed taking over transfer of the 4 demobilized Batt'ns all stores packed ready for Base	Cont'd
	16.2.18		Despatched to Base the most series of the 4 demobilized Batt'ns deficits complete to BHQ & BAOS 2nd Plank	Cont'd
	20.2.18		Return 25th Bn't winter depot	Cont'd
	21.2.18		Arrange for taking on surplus Baggage etc of 19th N. Fusiliers (Pioneer) Cont'd reorganization of this Batt'n	Cont'd
	24.2.18		Completes the reorganization of Pioneer Batt'n as far as AO Dept was concerned. Arranges with AODS 30th Div to take over 2	Cont'd

WAR DIARY
or
INTELLIGENCE SUMMARY.

Army Form C. 2118.

(Erase heading not required.)

Instructions regarding War Diaries and Intelligence Summaries are contained in F.S. Regs., Part II. and the Staff Manual respectively. Title pages will be prepared in manuscript.

Place	Date	Hour	Summary of Events and Information	Remarks and references to Appendices
La Motte	21.2.18		Divis. Salvage kept at Blaringhem and Doperinghe. Attended conference at Corps H.Q. re A.D.O.S. 2nd Corps.	Wus⁰
			D.A.D.O.S. called.	Wus⁰
	28.2.18		Principle items of work performed in Corps Shops during Feb 1918	
			Armourers Shop	
			Lewis Guns — overhauled & repaired — 63	
			Vickers — do — 9	
			Magazines Lewis Gun — do — 181	
			Rifles — do — 208	
			Pistols — do — 136	
			Bicycles — do — 152	
			Steel Helmets — do — 117	
			Gas Drums — do — 5	
			Lewis Gun Drums with new pattern Grips — 76	
			Lent offs removed from rifles — 740	Wus⁰
			Shoemakers Shop	
			Boots repaired — 530	
			Boots overhauled & packed for Base 1639	
			Tailors Shop	
			Suits repaired — 290	
			Garments do — 173	
			Garments overhauled & packed for Base 6300	Wus⁰ Murr
			Bags repaired — 59	Capt
			28/2/18	D.A.D.O.S. 35th Divn

DADOrdnance   WAR DIARY 1st-31st March 1918   Army Form C. 2118
35 Division   *or*   INTELLIGENCE SUMMARY

WO 2 5

Place	Date	Hour	Summary of Events and Information	Remarks and references to Appendices
	1/3/18	1-15pm	Ban on charge of 13/15th Bde R.F.A. condemned for Returning by G.O.C.	W
	2/3/18		Inspection of Salvage Bn.	W
	3/4/18		Visited Salvage Section in forward area. Salvage dumps at Vlamertinghe & Ypernghe	W
	5/3/18		Gave a lecture to Division on economy in Ordnance stores	W
	6/3/18		Visited ADOS 2nd Corps. AA & QMG visited office	W
	10/3/18		Visited Salvage dump at Vlamertinghe. In camp etc.	W
	15/3/18		2-Inch Stokes Mortar on charge of 106th T.M.B. destroyed by shell fire. Replacements demanded.	W
			Issued 106 T.M.B. with a 2-Inch Stokes Mortar	W
	16/3/18		Demanded 1 Stokes Mortar winter for 105 T.M.B. to replace one condemned	W
	17/3/18		Issued 105 T.M.B. with 1 Stokes Mortar winter	W
	18/3/18		Received orders to prepare to move.	W
	22/3/18			W
	23/3/18		Commenced move to rear area and cleared Salvage Section from forward area	W

WAR DIARY or INTELLIGENCE SUMMARY

Army Form C. 2118

(Erase heading not required.)

Place	Date	Hour	Summary of Events and Information	Remarks and references to Appendices
	24/5		Arrived in new area. Sent to Gun Park for 500 magazines.	W
	25/5		Guns being delivered also direct to units. Issued 10 x 105" Infy B Bns with 7 Lewis Guns each to replace casualties.	W
Le Sieck	26/5		Issued 13 Vickers Guns to 35" M.G.C. to replace losses.	W
	27/5		Issued 4 — do — do — do — do —	W
	28/5		Moved forward to Lookay will open sub office. Left platoon in rearward area	W
	29/5		Moved main office to Vignacourt awaited Battn officer at Bouquemaison underclothing for unit.	W
	30/5		Moved HQrs office to Vignacourt. Left details at Lookay to administer. 10MC arcs 201.Co Rout Teun.	
	31/5		Sent lorry to Bouquemaison to draw 700 pairs of socks & 2000 towels. SLC Sedgwick drew these articles and delivered same to units.	W

1875 Wt. W593/826 1,000,000 4/15 J.B.C. & A. A.D.S.S./Forms/C. 2118.

CAPTAIN.
D.A.D.O.S. 85TH DIVISION.

War Diary.

D.A.D. Ordce. 35th Divn.

Period. 1st to 30th April 1918.

Volume 2.

Army Form C. 2118

WAR DIARY
D.A.D. Ordnance
35th Division

INTELLIGENCE SUMMARY

1–30 April 1918

Place	Date	Hour	Summary of Events and Information	Remarks and references to Appendices
In the field	1/4/18		Visited Div. H.Qrs, where Office and Brigade was and the ordinary Ordnance clerks and storemen from Vignacourt to Querrieu. I left our workshops, Salvage Company at Vignacourt. Also our Divisional Reserves excepting two small supply of Gas Appliances to units also use.	Lieut?
do	2/4/18		Found whole of forward area free of Salvage so sent out three lorries with a Warrant Officer to collect as much as possible – sent three three lorries fully loaded with Salvaged Ordnance Stores to the rear dump at Vignacourt where they were sorted to the Panel by the Salvage Company. Further Salved 600 Blankets which were at once issued to units of this Div.n. Visited Divn's Stead Quarter. Remanded 15 Lewis Guns for the 105th Inf. Brigade to replace losses by units.	Lieut?
do	3/4/18		Visited Div H.Q then on to Railhead which was changed during the morning so Rear dump to see Salvage Co and workshops also to bring forward Gas Appliances. Visited our Staff Captains also Seven Co's to find out immediate wants of Divn in I found certain my articles of our units portable equipment very little extra had to be demanded from Base.	Lieut?

WAR DIARY
or
INTELLIGENCE SUMMARY

(Erase heading not required.)

Army Form C. 2118

Instructions regarding War Diaries and Intelligence Summaries are contained in F.S. Regs., Part II. and the Staff Manual respectively. Title Pages will be prepared in manuscript.

Place	Date	Hour	Summary of Events and Information	Remarks and references to Appendices
Lutterfield	4.4.18		Frame the 15 Heavy Guns required to complete the 105th Inf. Brigade. Completed this with our Plankets required. Visited Bde HQ, Staff Capt. 35th Bde RA also Rear depot, dist/n etc. Benender 4 Heavy Guns for the 12th H.L.J	Law J
	5.4.18		Visited Bde HQ then to Rear before. Arranged with Roo for an Salved Site to stow away from view account of ADOS Corps HQ reference Oil – obtained on required	Law J
	6.4.18		Visited G.O.C. 104th Inf.Brigade also Co.s – Visited D.I.T.O. and Rear depot. Salving going on ahead and being evacuated daily. Arranged Salvage Co. to visit local villages where troops have been billeted to search canal sites etc:	Law J
	7.4.18		Visited Bde HQ then to Nieuland and Rear depot. Pt out 31st working well and are unfair demands upon Same has been met.	Law J
	8.4.18		Visited Bde HQ also Railhead. Benender by unfair wire 1500 Complete change S.D, Shirt, drawers, socks to meet the Corps and this scheme to dealing wire Mustard Gas Cases.	Law J
	10.4.18		Moved Advanced depot and office to Steenvoorde under Canvas. Visited Bde HQ also ADOS Corps and workshop.	Law J
	11.4.18		Visited Bde HQ then to Railhead to see Roo as to drawing and also evacuation of ordnance Stores. Some 10 railway Steel' or Canvas damage done.	Law J

Place	Date	Hour	Summary of Events and Information	Remarks and references to Appendices
Intelpices	12/4/18		Visited Dir Itre - Raithea and Wardstafa. Found site to Wardstafa. his Reserves etc at Talwan. Arranged with the R.O. to find Points for Salvage Company near to Belle Eglise. 1 wagon and limber 18 pdr QF to A/157 to replace one destroyed by hostile shell fire.	[illeg.]
	13/4/18		Visited Rea depot - Stated Salvage Co by was to Belle Eglise at 9.30 - return for Packs etc. Visited DADOS Coles re Band - sent same by was to Enthomer 11 a.m. with lorry for Slides etc. Same withdrawn and Reserves to Talwan. Went to Army Gun Park to try Vickers Guns for 35th M.G. Batts - drew Same and Same was [?] unit. Visited Dir Itre reported moves all clear.	[illeg.]
	14.4.18		Visited Dir Itre - Raithea also C.O. 18th HLI reference Company Ammunt Cooker destroyed by Shell fire. The 1500 duds etc Shelter writer to arrived - 200 sent to 35th Batt. Office & 1300 to Rear depot. Visited ADOS Coles re Signs to Leins trenches. Saw issues for Anti Air Craft Pompoms - Present-type being withdrawn. Journey demanded to West Lorries, 3 lorries, 1 fire E.S. Wagon, 1 Drain, 1 ore Patrim Travelling Kitchen to 17th Royal Scots, Cooker Complete Turn-out to 1/9 St's, [illeg.] for 15th HLI, 1 Kitchen Travelling for 15th Cheshires. (Replaces 20/4/18)	[illeg.]

WAR DIARY
or
INTELLIGENCE SUMMARY

Army Form C. 2118

Place	Date	Hour	Summary of Events and Information	Remarks and references to Appendices
Rafiu	15/5/18		Visits six heavy guns issued to the Div is in - inspecting the Infty Units Dup per Painters. Visited Div Stp, Railhead, Staff Capt R.A., workshops Salvage dump - Also A.D.O.S 5th Corps. Received 1 heavy gun for 17 Royal Scots to replace unserviceable one.	(aus)f
	16ª		Authorized receiving. Visited Div Stp - Railhead and Staffs. Demanded 1 water cart for 18 heavies to complete also one to H.M. Staffs. Demanded 1 G.S. limber for H.E. Brens Steel Time Visited Div Stp etc. Demanded 1 18 pr. Q.F. Gun for A/157 to replace one for serv use	(aus)f (aus)f
	20ª			(aus)f
	21*		Arr slung visited depot.	(aus)f
	22ª		A.D.O.S 5th Corps visited depot.	(aus)f
	23ª		Visited Div Stp - Railhead etc. Issued new 18 pdr to A/157.	(aus)f
	24		Visited A.D.O.S v Corps reviewed Cadre - Then to workshops Div Stp and Railhead. Clear'd all Salvage dumps and transmitted all Stores to B rae.	(aus)f
	25		Visited the Railhead also Dn Salvage Dump; Worked Div. H.Q; sent lorry to Corps H.Q for French Shelters for DADMS; Rang up ADOS 5th Corps reference winter clothing being returned & this Div. nothing to return the second blanket, leather jerkins + coats sheep skin lined till May 18th instead of hand-ing them in on the 1st May. this is being referred to higher authority. Walter Rattles	(aus)f —

WAR DIARY
or
INTELLIGENCE SUMMARY
(Erase heading not required.)

Army Form C. 2118

Place	Date	Hour	Summary of Events and Information	Remarks and references to Appendices
In the Field	25/4/18 cont	1	Waterborrto to ascertain progress of Baths for Mustard Gas. Watlow - visited the Pioneers. Visited my Div. Workshops at Talmas - work progressing well. 3410 Howells Mway & Protectors rec'd from Base - arranged that Coys report to have some fitted by my armourer.	Ans 1
	26		Two Lewis Guns for 17th Sherwoods test on raid. Visited Div. HQ - railhead - Rest Salvage Dumps. Visited Workshops. Prepared statement on Winter Clothing for Dist HQ giving suggested additions & deletions. Four Lorries sent to Dumps to collect. Having reduced the heavy demands by Units for Wheels Poles Drag Rs. etc. as also Jr. have written to HQ suggesting that a qualified NCO be attached to my unit whose sole duty will be to inspect and finally pass all articles condemned by Unit Transport Officers. The two Gas rattles for Battery for R.A. arrived from Base and issued to Units.	Ans 2
	27	x	Visited Q HQ - railhead - workshops. Then to HQ 35th Div. Wing to arrange with the O.C. to administer them for Ordnance Supplies.	Ans 3
	28		Visited Div. HQ - Railhead. Workshops, also advanced Salvage Dumps. Arranged for Transport to clear same. Two Lewis Guns for 15th Sherwoods arrived and issued. Two Lewis Guns complete, test by 19th D.L.I. - 2 demanded from Gun Park to replace.	Ans 4
	29		Visited Q HQ - Railhead - Salvage Co. - also Workshops. Visited OC Div-train on the subject of surplus transport in the Divn also as to demands from units for Wagons guyO ment. Two Lewis Guns for 19th D.L.I. discharged by shell fire - demand sent to Gun Park. Lewis Guns complete demanded for Pte. N.Z. (Pioneers under authority A.O. T.	Ans 5

800 3/14 25.4.18.

Visited D HQ

Army Form C. 2118

WAR DIARY
or
INTELLIGENCE SUMMARY
(Erase heading not required.)

Instructions regarding War Diaries and Intelligence Summaries are contained in F. S. Regs., Part II. and the Staff Manual respectively. Title Pages will be prepared in manuscript.

Place	Date	Hour	Summary of Events and Information	Remarks and references to Appendices
In the Field	30/9/16		Visited D H Q - 400 Packs wanted for turning purposes whilst (Pursers as on rest) Visited Railhead - Salvage Dumps. Saw Corps Salvage Officer and arranged to take over today the Salvage Dump in Toutencourt. Also arranged for Div Salvage Officers to attend an Ammunition Course at an Ordnance Dept. Tested Rear depôt and Workshops. Tested Poole Gun Park at Carlaut also I.O.M. Shore & No 1 Mobile Workshops reference the repair of Telescopic Glasses &c. Principal items of work performed in Divi Workshops during the Month Armourers Shops	
			M/c Guns Lewis repaired and overhauled = 31. Pistols repaired and overhauled = 5	
			" Vickers " " " = 14. Primus Stoves " " = 6	
			Magazines Lewis Gun " " = 72. Lamps Braying " " = 2	
			Rifles " " = 516. Torches Electric " " = 7	
			Bayonets Scabbards " " = 105. Clinometers " " = 1	
			Hotchkiss Guns " " = 1 Bicycles " " = 91.	
			Steel Helmets " " = 382.	
			Bootmaking Shops	
			Boots repaired and reissued = 650 pairs	
			" examined, tarred, and £. 779. L. Austin Moses	
			bagged for Base Captain	
			D. A. D. O. S.	
			35d Div'n Gros	

War Diary.
D.A.D. Ord^{ce}. 35th Divⁿ.

Period May 1st to 31st 1918.

Volume ii.

WAR DIARY or INTELLIGENCE SUMMARY

Army Form C. 2118

DeADOrdnance 35 Division
1 – 31 May 1916

Place	Date	Hour	Summary of Events and Information	Remarks and references to Appendices
In the Field	1/5/16	–	Visited A.H.Q. – Railhead also Salvage Dumps. Visited Rear Depot. D.D.O.S. 3rd Army went A.D.O.S. 5th Corps visited Depot. One 6" T.M. belonging to X/35 examined. New one demanded to replace.	W
	2/5/16	–	Visited D.H.Q. – Railhead & Salvage Dumps. Visited Rear Depot also ADOS 5th Corps. Drew & Issued Numbering for trial with Vickers Guns from OO & GPO Troops.	W
	3/5/16	–	Visited Div. H.Q. – Railheads – Fortencourt Salvage Dump also A.D.O.S. 5th Corps. 6" T.M. for X/35 arrived. Warloy Salvage Dump cleared, & men sent to Herissart.	W
	4/5/16	–	Visited @ H.Q. – Visited Despatch Officers reference the underclothing of the Divn. Arranged with R.O.O. Bell Eglise that all stores to Acheville could go from there – also that all underclothing asked should go to one Dept. thereat in Toutencourt. Visited Div. Salvage Dumps at Feéle Eglise, Toutencourt, Herissart. Drew Hos Issued Anti Gas Bottles from the O.O. 5th Corps. Field Railhead at Roile – as a result I arranged for all stores for B.E.W., other than returned timber, clothing to go from Belle Eglise.	W
	5/5/16	–	Visited Rear Depot & Rouse & Railhead. Div. H.Q. Claims Officer – O.C. 232 Employ. Co. – Salvage Officer & Dumps. Sent an Armr. Staff Sgt. to Army Gun Park at Candas to give temp. help. Special Golf Bag shaped carrier for Lewis Guns demanded, one New for Btty, Baths & The Toneur Bath. Unit informed by D.A.Q.M.G.	W

Fisher

WAR DIARY
or
INTELLIGENCE SUMMARY
(Erase heading not required.)

Army Form C. 2118

Place	Date	Hour	Summary of Events and Information	Remarks and references to Appendices
Field	6/5/16	1	Visited Rear Depot for supply of moulds etc. Medal ribbon for the Corps Commander's parade. Visited O.E.Q. also Salvage Dumps at Belle Eglise, Toutencourt + Herissart. Took the new Salvage Officer under instruction with me. Visited E.O. M/c D.C. I also E.O. rather on general Ordnance question. All Cycles lost during retirement replaced with Units to day. Visited O.E. No 3 + Co 35 Div Train re Wagon Equipt. Also O.E. 35 D.A.C. regarding the issue of boots to his Unit & the return of worn pairs to Ordnance.	Unused
	7/5/16	1	Visited to 26 Q - Railhead Road. Railhead Belle Eglise. Salvage Dumps at Belle Eglise, Toutencourt + Herissart. Arranged for a New Salvage Dump on Herissart - this section to also work Raclempré. Visited Rear Depot. Baton packs for Div Instruction arrived for issue.	Unused
	8/5/16	1	Visited Div H.Q. Visited Div Dump at Albeville also all Salvage Dumps. At Belle Eglise Dump found a lot of graduates stored which I arranged to be filed over till tomorrow when I could know just what is required for this Div.	Unused
	9/5/16	1	Visited O.E.H.Q. Demanded 4.5 stem carriage 105 to replace one damaged by shell fire. Obtained 6 Renberg, 11 Engraved, 4 Pilots, 4 graddings, 1 Telescopic, 18 pairs Formoculars. 1y Visited from Salvage Dump Belle Eglise. Visited also Salvage Dump at Toutencourt + Herissart. Saw the OC 35 N.E.C. re general Order matters especially regarding Livery indents received today concerning which I report is going to D.H.Q.	Unused
	10/5/16	1	Esplan : Bells .P.O.D. reported from O.E.C. Train for learning one condemned for hoarse .... Pai show. 1 17 pdr gun only demanded for 35/109. In place Trans under instruction of PDOS. Visited O.E.H.Q. with Coy Bills A.O.D then to Salvage Dumps Toutencourt where I arranged for lorries to pick up Salvage here for Belle Eglise. Visited also Belle Eglise + Herissart dumps taking Salvage Officer with me. Saw E.O. 35 N.S.C. further about his indents also E.O. Div Train as to the best way of finding any surplus to Establishment Transport in the DivZ. Visited Rear Depot. and	Unused

Army Form C. 2118

WAR DIARY
or
INTELLIGENCE SUMMARY

(Erase heading not required.)

Instructions regarding War Diaries and Intelligence Summaries are contained in F.S. Regs., Part II. and the Staff Manual respectively. Title Pages will be prepared in manuscript.

Place	Date	Hour	Summary of Events and Information	Remarks and references to Appendices
Field	10/5/18 cont.	-	and workshops explained the working to Capt Mills.	
	11/5/18	-	Visited CO 35 Div Wing re undercla Pump baths, cooking stoves 5°. Visited D.H.Q. & Bell Eglise Salvage	W
	12/5/18	-	Visited D.H.Q; Salvage Dumps at Bell Eglise, Herissart, + Toutencourt. Arranged to have the Wood between Toutencourt + Acquens salvaged. Anglo training not yet arrived. Toutencourt Rear Depot	2 and 3
	13/5/18	-	Carriage for D/159 arrived. Visited D.H.Q, also all Salvage Dumps. Capt Mills (A.D) attached mainly for Duty in India. Visited O.C 35th N.T.C also 6% workshops re paint, timber 5°.	2 and 3
			Visited Rear depot + shops; 7 G.T. Wagon loads of Wood found on road.	
	14/5/18	-	Visited D.H.Q. - railhead + Salvage Dumps; A.D.O.S. v. Capts visited Depot, also Workshops	2 and 3
	14[?]/18	-	Visited Bde workshops + Salvage Dumps Rear Depot. Then to 10 of 3rd Army + P. Workshops	2 and 3
	15/5/18	-	Visited D.H.Q - railhead + salvage Dumps - A.D.O.S v Capts visited Depot - also Workshops	2 and 3
	16/5/18	-	Visited D.H.Q. - also Salvage Dumps at Herissart, Toutencourt & Bell Eglese. Visited T.P.O. Authorised + obtained 18 Revolvers - 12 for this Divr + 6 for 38 Divr (Removed 6 T.P. to replace no destroyed by shell fire.	2 and 3
	17/5/18	-	Visited D.H.Q. - Railheads - also all Salvage Dumps. Visited O.C Brickine - 18 hrs of D/159 arrived for issuing.	2 and 3
	18/5/18	-	Visited D.H.Q. also Railhead Salvage Dumps. Visited C.R.A + Staff Captain re Gun Slides	W
	19/5/18	-	Lt. Vard Dth Salvage Officer left for Engles to go before the Standing Medical Board for further classification. Visited D.H.Q. also Salvage Dumps in Herissart. Visited G.O.C. 105 L & Bde -	and 5
	19/5/18	-	also Staff Capt + C.O. of Brigade re the return of Timber Stores.	
	20/5	-	Visited Div H.Q. Railheads - Salvage Dumps. Visited C.O. 1st Sherwoods. also Rear Depot Workshops. Capt Mills left for England on completion of tour of duty. Arranged to move Salvage Dumps from Herissart + Toutencourt to Harponville -- Visited	and

WAR DIARY
or
INTELLIGENCE SUMMARY.
(Erase heading not required.)

Army Form C. 2118.

Instructions regarding War Diaries and Intelligence Summaries are contained in F. S. Regs., Part II. and the Staff Manual respectively. Title pages will be prepared in manuscript.

Place	Date	Hour	Summary of Events and Information	Remarks and references to Appendices
Field	21/5/18		Visited Our HQ. Sent car to Boulogne to bring back Col Farmar arranged with DADOS 38 Divn to take over 4 German Guns issued to this division for instructional purposes. Sent long hot fortnights due to this Divn from O.O. 3rd Army to A.D.O.S. 5th Corps asking if they could be handed as they are now urgently required my Divn having gone back into the line. Railhead advised if I am today; great saving as it enables me to distribute stores to Units during the dan day. Arranged with Staff Captain 10/- off Bde that he can have 50 sets of SD clothing at 13/- HQ to deal with any cases of Mustard Gas. Also arranged for men in the line to have clean socks every third day these being drawn by Units from the Divl Baths Officer direct instead of having to come to me	Fourth
	22/5/18		Demand 6" T.M. + Bed for X 35 T.M. 13. To replace one destroyed by Shell Fire. Tested O to Q - Railhead. Salvage to also with Salvage Officer to Tinqueville to cart new Dumps. GOC with the aa QMG + ADC visited Rear Depot and Workshops - men were all doing their hours work well top separator at time of work. Salved 250 Wahl lens urgently needed for Units in the line - - - - - - -	VaisJ
	23/5/18		Visited Rear Depot Tent thought 100 suits urgently required to combat Mustard Gas - took same to Sedainville. Visited DHQ- also Railhead + Salvage Office Tested Staff Depot (Salvage) 5 Corps reference area Salved a further 100 Water Iron for use of Units on the line. Handed over the 4 German Machine Guns	VaisJ

Army Form C. 2118.

WAR DIARY
or
INTELLIGENCE SUMMARY.
(Erase heading not required.)

Instructions regarding War Diaries and Intelligence Summaries are contained in F. S. Regs., Part II. and the Staff Manual respectively. Title pages will be prepared in manuscript.

Place	Date	Hour	Summary of Events and Information	Remarks and references to Appendices
23/5/18 Corps Field	23/5/18		Guns to D.A.D.O.S. 36 Divn - These are for instruction of Divisions out of the Line. Told O.C. Salvage to move his H.Q. to Hazonville leaving 12 men & 1 Engineer who will be attached to Corps Belle Eglise for Rations &c.	Lewis
	24/5/18		Visited Q.H.Q. - Railhead - Rectory. Demanded 1 Vickers Guns for 35th N.F.C. discharged shell fires. Demanded 1 Barrel for 3" Stokes for 105 T.M.B.	Lewis
	25/5/18		Visited D.H.Q. - also Salvage Dumps at Hazonville + Belle Eglise. Visited A.D.O.S. 59? reference special demand of Tables + forms for med stations on salvaged. Visited Sent 3rd Army H.N. Workshops.	Lewis
	26/5/18		Demanded 36 Lewis Guns vide OV/33 of 27/5/18 completing units to 24 Guns for the line. Visited Q.H.Q., A.D.O.S. v Corps + Major Hing A.D.O. Visited the Depot. Cold Hell. A.A.M.G., C.R.A. Visited the Depot.	Lewis
	27/5/18		Visited H.Q. 35th Divn with A.D.O.S. 35th Corps + Major Hing A.D.O. Saw Col Var- man Asst A.A.M.G. re the confidential report on Captain Mills A.S.O. as to his suitability for an appointment as (A.)A.D.O.S. Visited Railhead at Belle Eglise. The Gas Officer 35th Divn gave a lecture to the detachment on the Mustard Gas question.	Lewis
	28/5/18		Visited Divn H.Q. Demanded one Lewis Gun not Report for 17th Lanc. Forces to replace one lost. 36 Lewis Guns received - thus completing the units to 24 Lewis Guns for Batts exclusive of the Hallowed for A.A. v on A.P. work.	Lewis
	29/5/18		Started in two days refresher course on the Hotchkiss Guns at my Depot for the benefit of the Div Train. Divn H.T.C. Divn Supply C. Visited Divn H.Q.	Lewis

Army Form C. 2118.

WAR DIARY
or
INTELLIGENCE SUMMARY.
(Erase heading not required.)

Instructions regarding War Diaries and Intelligence Summaries are contained in F. S. Regs., Part II. and the Staff Manual respectively. Title pages will be prepared in manuscript.

Place	Date	Hour	Summary of Events and Information	Remarks and references to Appendices
Field	29/3/18 Cont	-	1.18004 Guns & Carriage 13/187 Condemned - renewal wired for. Wired Gun Park for Tripod & Mounting MK IV + 10 Barrels Victors Guns for 35 R.E. Visited Salvage Dumps with DADMG. Visited Rear Depot + workshops at Talmas.	Vas[?]
	30/3/18	-	Discharges Rifle demanded from Base to complete Divn up to establishment of 96 per Infy Battn. Visited D.H.Q. Visited Belle Eglise Railhead - arranged for the Salvage Staff (12 men) to move to new Railhead at Caunchenes where they will be fed by R.O.O. all other men are now at Tongueville with forward Dumps at Gentis. Visited R.O.O. Authent where I obtained 19 Revolvers + 96 frs Batts. Tondlers, Hotchkiss refused another convoy. Visited R.W. Rail also Rear Depot workshops. Visited ADOS 5th Corps on General Ordnance Matters. Visited O.C French Mission on the question of helping to remove civilians from forward shelled areas - promised to let all I visited into returning lorries &c.	Vas[?]
	31/3/18	-	Visited D.H.Q. & Salvage Dumps at Haysenville. Visited C.O. 14th D.L.I. also R.E. stores of 7 Lancs, 18 Lancs + 9/5 D.L.I. - found no stocks being held. all men attacked from the Div Employ Coy, informed of the ADMS. Visited Rear Depot and Shops - then to 3rd Army Gun Park for Barrels urgently required by 35th R.E. to Y.O.M. 3rd Army S.N. Workshops for Shombos Horn Cylinders.	Vas[?]

Army Form C. 2118.

WAR DIARY
or
INTELLIGENCE SUMMARY.
(Erase heading not required.)

Place	Date	Hour	Summary of Events and Information	Remarks and references to Appendices
Field	31/5/18		Principal items of Work performed in my Workshops during the Month:—	
			Armourers Shops:—	
			M/c Guns Tests, repaired + overhauled = 60 Bayonets Scabbards repaired & handles = 36	
			" Vickers " " = 4 Pistols " = 44	
			Magazines Lewis Gun " = 44 Steel Helmets " = 78	Appx Q
			Hotchkiss Guns " = 2 Primus Stoves " = 11	
			Rifles " = 270 Bicycles " = 101	
			Boot Shops:—	
			No. of Ankle Boots repaired & re-issued = 647 pairs	
			" " " overhauled, repaired, & sent to Base = 2c 30 pairs	
			Tailor Shops	
			180 pairs Puttees overhauled; 120 pairs were made serviceable for issue.	

L. Awatson Sharer
Captain
DADOS 35th Division

WAR DIARY D.A.D. Ordnance.
35 Division.
1st to 30th June 1918.

Army Form C. 2118.

INTELLIGENCE SUMMARY

Place	Date	Hour	Summary of Events and Information	Remarks and references to Appendices
Field	1/6/18	-	Demanded 1 Vickers Gun for 35 M.G.C. to replace one destroyed by shell fire. Visited D.H.Q. Then to R.O.O. Ronchérat. - Recd. Salvage Situation and Deficiency Return ie: Officers and Mans Dumps at Haynonville sent over at Ronchérat, on 5th Corps Dump, and one man at Road for Railhead evacuation work.	Paw P
	2/6/18	-	Visited Railheads D.H.Q. Visited O.C. French Mission re transportation of Civilians to back area.	Paw S
	3/6/18	-	Demanded 1 Lewis Gun for 19th D.C.L.I. to replace one destroyed by shell fire. Visited O.HQ, also Salvage dumps at Haynonville & Ranchérat. Visited R.O.O. Road also Staff Captain Salvage V Corps. Visited A.O.C. 1st Sept. Who also C.O. 19th D.L.I. Gun demanded 1/6/18 for 35th M.G.C. arrived today. 35th M.G.C. completed with scale of 32 per gun of H.G. Belts.	(Paw S
	4/6/18	-	Visited D.H.Q. - Visited Divl Gas Baths. Visited O.C. Salvage at Haynonville. Demanded 11 Lewis Guns complete less Magazines for 18th Lan Fus to replace those lost in the action of Aveluy Wood. Guns demanded for 19th @ D.C.L.I. 3/6/18 recd today.	(Paw P
	5/6/18	-	The 11 Guns demanded for 18th L.F arrived. Visited Div H.Q. & Salvage Dumps - Railhead + Div Shops at Talmas. A.D.O.S. 5th Corps visited the Depôt. Demanded Magazines for 19th F to replace those destroyed by Shell Fire.	Paw P
	6/6/18	-	14 A.A. Mountings arrived. A.D.A.Q.M.G. visited Depôt.	Paw S

Army Form C. 2118.

WAR DIARY
or
INTELLIGENCE SUMMARY.
(Erase heading not required.)

Place	Date	Hour	Summary of Events and Information	Remarks and references to Appendices
Field	7/6/18	-	Visited Div HQ - Railhead - Salvage Dumps & rear Depot. Demanded 1 Vickers to replace one destroyed by shell fire.	Laus?
	8/6/18	-	Visited D.H.Q. - salvage dumps - rear depot.	Laus?
	9/6/18	-	Visited D.H.Q. - Rear Depot - Railhead - Salvage Dumps. Demanded 1 Vickers Gun to replace one destroyed by shell fire. Demanded 1 Vickers Gun to replace one destroyed by shell fire (2 altogether). 18 pdr Carriage & 9/157 bar. demanded - new one demanded to replace.	Laus?
	10/6/18	-	Visited D.H.Q - Salvage Dumps - Railhead - Rear Depot also visited OC Div. Mun.	Laus?
	11/6/18	-	Visited Div HQ - E.R.A Burdon - E.O. 157 Bde R.F.A. E.O. 19 K @ L.S - also visited Salvage Dumps & Railhead. Visited Rear Depot & work-shops. Arranged with ADOS for special issue of barrels to 35 M.G.C. in anticipation of worn out ones in covering roading party.	Laus?
	12/6/18	-	Demanded a further 4 Lewis Guns for Battn (i.e. 36 in all bringing them up to scale F. Demanded 19 Barrels for 35 M.G.C. to replace unserviceable. Demanded 1 Vickers Gun only to replace one destroyed by shell fire. ADOS 5th Corps visited the Depot also the Rear Depot & Workshops. 18/pr Gun and	Laus?

WAR DIARY
~~INTELLIGENCE~~ SUMMARY.
(Erase heading not required.)

Army Form C. 2118.

Place	Date	Hour	Summary of Events and Information	Remarks and references to Appendices
Field	12 cont.	-	and carriage belonging to 13/157 R.F.A. destroyed by Hostile Shell fire. New sights only: replacement demanded.	
	13/6	-	Visited D.H.Q. - Salvage Dump. - C.O. 19. D.L.I. - OC 35 Div Wing + OC 35. M.T.C. The H Lewis Guns required to bring Divr up to Scale. Fired today also rec'd all pouches due for carrying the Dischargers Grenade. The new glasses magnifying hand also received. Visited OC 3rd Army H.V. Workshops with 12 Binoculars & Chronometers &c for repair.	Paus⊙ /
	14/6	-	Vickers Gun for 3rd N.F. received - visited D.H.Q. - Railhead & Salvage Officer. Rec'd warning notice of a move & arranged to visit DADOS of other Divns tomorrow. Wired Staff Capt (Salvage) Corps re Salvage to movements.	Paus⊙ /
	15/6	-	Visited D.H.Q. - was shown a memo by Col Farman to the effect that The G.O.C. was putting my name forward as being suitable for the appointment of an A.D.O.S. Visited Salvage Officer also Railhead Rear Depot. Visited the DADOS 12 Divn and made arrangements to hand over my forward depot to him on 16/6. I am not taking over his depot but going to a place near same but far more suitable. Arranged with Salvage Officer to meet the Salvage Officer 12 Divn & to complete all details of handing	Paus⊙ /

Army Form C. 2118.

WAR DIARY
or
INTELLIGENCE SUMMARY.
(Erase heading not required.)

Instructions regarding War Diaries and Intelligence Summaries are contained in F.S. Regs., Part II. and the Staff Manual respectively. Title pages will be prepared in manuscript.

Place	Date	Hour	Summary of Events and Information	Remarks and references to Appendices
Field	15/5	—	Handing over our Salvage Dumps &c. Tasked C.O. 106 Field Ambce & inspected Q.M. Stores &c. Have arranged to have works, hope, in present situation in Salinas till move is completed.	W
	16/5	—	Started at 5 am with ADOS 5th Corps to visit No 11 Ordce Depot but car broke down at 6.40 am & trip had to be abandoned. Tasked D.H.Q. Then to site of new depot where the tent sides were settled - started to move the detachment. Arranged with OC 35 M.T.C. for two special lorries to clear the Salvage Co. from Haynecourt. Fixed up all the Town Salvage dump sides with the Salvage Officer as follows:- (1) H.Q. 1 Officer & 23 O.R. at Erinchevral Shed 57 D N12 c 6.4. (2) 1 NCO & 6 men at Pigeons " " D.0.14. B5.7. (3) 1 " 6 " " Puchvillers " " N22 c.3.1. (4) 1 " 6 " " Beauquesne " " N2 d.1.8. The Salvage Officer instructed to make arrangements for each of parties 2,3 & 4 to be rationed locally.	Reus V
	17/5	—	Visited DHQ. Took down all tentage & moved to new depot at 12 noon. Tasked 5 D.A. S.O. Tasked DADOS & Dire re Ants Gas Appliances & changed Tasked Div Salvage Co. & saw all clear from old Depot at Haynecourt. Saw Town Major reference the local water supply.	Reus V

Army Form C. 2118.

WAR DIARY
or
INTELLIGENCE SUMMARY.
(Erase heading not required.)

Instructions regarding War Diaries and Intelligence Summaries are contained in F. S. Regs., Part II. and the Staff Manual respectively. Title pages will be prepared in manuscript.

Place	Date	Hour	Summary of Events and Information	Remarks and references to Appendices
Field	18/6	–	Visited O.H.Q. – also Salvage Officer who explained to him the necessity of building up a reserve of 370 Petrol Tins, also of using all his dumps daily. Visited Railhead & rear shops – – – – – –	(aus)t
	19/6	–	Visited Div. H.Q. – took Capt Grenshell to 10th Corps. (Demanded 1. 180th for G/159 to replace 18pdr Gun No.4117 condemned for boring. Demanded 1 Lewis Gun for 17th Royal Scots to replace one destroyed by shell fire.	(aus)t
	20/6	–	Visited O.H.Q. A.D.O.S. 1st Corps. visited Depot and saw Lt Dawson re a transfer to the R.O.Dept. for Lt Dawson of the 19th N.F. Visited with A.D.O.S. 1st Corps D.L. 35th D.A.C. & inspected the ammunition of all sections. The Chief Clerk & 2 W.O's gone to C.E. & went P.K.O. leaving me with 1 W.O. & a TyClerk to run the whole Ord. Ord. Services. Visited C.O's 17th & C.O. 18th D.S. & also Staff Captain 104th & 118th. A.A.D.V.S. visited the Depot	
	21/6	–	Visited D.H.Q. also Salvage Officer. Visited Rear Depot – Workshops & Railhead. O.C. 35th Div. French Museum to see me reference the Salving of some valuable French records etc. from the village of Maillet Maillet. Demanded 180th gun has been Buck belongs to 1/3/157	

A7092 Wt. W125 9/Mr2923 750,000. 1/17. D. D. & I. Ltd. Forms/C2118/14

Army Form C. 2118.

WAR DIARY
or
INTELLIGENCE SUMMARY.
(Erase heading not required.)

Place	Date	Hour	Summary of Events and Information	Remarks and references to Appendices
Field	21/6 Cont		B/157 to replace one condemned for scoring. Cancelled my leave owing to shortage of N.C.Os – Arranged with Salvage Officer for four men to report there daily to help in store houses – 3 storemen also being sick with Trench Fever	
	22/6/18		3" Stoke T.M. destroyed by shell fire – new one demanded for lost Pdr. Visited D.H.Q – Visited Salvage Co. & arranged for Salvage Officer to visit the Soldier Hand in the Div Area & to report to me to learn how many men D[?] it will take to work there. Visited ADOS & Corps on Genl Ord. matters. Mentioned Service Medal awarded to G/Bdr Glo Marshall R.F.a attached to this Unit. Made final arrangements with Pte 3510 French River to take valuable French records & Church goods from the village of Nailly Maillet at 4 am tomorrow 23.6.8. Motld Tailors shop from Rear Depot to Forward Depot. D.A.Q.M.G. visited the Depot.	
	23/6/18		Visited Nailly Maillet at 4 am with Lorries & cleared much Church property, books, pictures &c, also records, furniture &c of French people very grateful. Visited D.H.Q, 3rd Army T.O.M, 3rd Army at Anti reference Binoculars	Three

WAR DIARY
or
INTELLIGENCE SUMMARY.
(Erase heading not required.)

Army Form C. 2118.

Place	Date	Hour	Summary of Events and Information	Remarks and references to Appendices
Field	23/10	—	Three WO's still ill — great assistance given to me by the Pondon Stone & Thompson. The Cooks are doing WO's work.	
	24/10	—	Visited DHQ — Salvage Dumps also went into the Soldiers question. Other Dumps appear to be meeting the situation on our area — reported situation to R5 also wrote to Staff Capt Salvage on this point. Visited Rear Depot — very hard pressed as owing to illness only 4 Am^ns are available for work.	
	25/10	—	Visited DHQ — also Salvage Officer Dumps — Visited Gas Coy offt Bde reference tentage. Also CO 35 MT G Batts ref Escorts of NCOs. Visited OC 35 Div Wing also Man depot & workshops.	
	26/10	—	Visited DHQ — AA & QMG granted me leave from tomorrow — arranged that Capt Warrington 19th DLI should answer for me whilst I am away. Lent Car to CO 19th DLI to take him to Boulogne.	
	27/10	—	1 Vickers Gun demanded to replace one condemned.	
	29	—	1 Vickers Gun for 35 MGC received — Visited DAQMG re move. Visited Rear Depot & issued instructions re move to new area; arranged details for move of Salvage Co	

Army Form C. 2118.

WAR DIARY
or
INTELLIGENCE SUMMARY.
(Erase heading not required.)

Place	Date	Hour	Summary of Events and Information	Remarks and references to Appendices
Field	30/6		Commenced move Rear Depot stores &c to new area. Light car reported at Q.M.Q. for employment re move	
	29/6/17		Worked with Q Pork (Capt Hamel) re Soldes Huts at Beau- geve (Bezure) Engineers Rechwelere (Lather sloping S.S type) all erected by 35st C.P.C. also Ramchent in use by 63? Dron — included Ord. Salvage Officer.	

G.O. Warnington
Captain
for ODADOS
35st Dron

War Diary.

D.A.D.O.S. 35 British Divn

Period 1st to 31st July 1918

Volume 2.

Army Form C. 2118.

WAR DIARY
or
INTELLIGENCE SUMMARY
(Erase heading not required.)

WN 27

Place	Date	Hour	Summary of Events and Information	Remarks and references to Appendices
Field	1/8		Left Beauguesne at 8.30 am with 4 Lorries and arrived at Thezernes at 3.45 pm and billeted at Gondardenne. Visited D.HQ who instructed that HQ tomorrow would be at Oudezeele and 25 salvage personnel would report with Lorry at 9.15 am tomorrow. Both Workshops reported arrival by train at Argues	U
	2/10		Left Gondardenne at 9.40 am with 4 Lorries; 25 salvage men arrived without a lorry - it was arranged with D.H.Q to send back a lorry for them this afternoon - with one for the Div Workshops at Argues. Arrived Oudezeele 2 pm - salvage & workshops arrived 7 pm. Steel 27 Tuag 4.	U
	3/10		Rec'd message by phone from Roubrugge that 3 huts of Depot stores had arrived - lorries sent out to clear.	U.
	4-7/10		Landed for sites in use now for Depôt; but found Haven neither under Sylvestre; ascertained French troops, a wound for a few days. Rex required improved England	U

Army Form C. 2118.

WAR DIARY
or
INTELLIGENCE SUMMARY.
(Erase heading not required.)

Place	Date	Hour	Summary of Events and Information	Remarks and references to Appendices
Field	5.7.18		Started receiving tenners Rafah which train [illegible] that down at 2 pm, up to which time only them which had been disarmed, called at Suez left a telephone for R.S.O. can visit his booking arrived at 4 pm. Found Rafah visit well, informed "J.a. again. decided on A.A.&Q.M.G. H.Q. who arranged return car & [illegible] visit & we would start making arrangements for Infantry of 30th Division to entrain which are at Katatba. A.A.&Q.M.G. visit rail at [illegible] morning later. joined and train here at 39/1 Py to 1.2 & to arranged by train to join their greet train.	[illegible]
	6.7.18		Visited railway Kitchen, found that standing to railway staff saw S/S Sams & S/S Kieser, he was up looking for officers, he had dug [illegible] on a triangle. On washing we Rafah found that Sergt & Bar did to look after accounts etc. found that A.A.&Q.M.G. had called & told the accounts staff the was now in his Barracks. Decided on alterations which were to be established, 35 Dist train but required my clearing at P14 a 19 allowed to except but announced that by evening they visited D.H.Q. twice, completed [illegible] D.A.A.G. was [illegible] information to the communicated. (continued overleaf)	[illegible]

WAR DIARY
or
INTELLIGENCE SUMMARY.

(Erase heading not required.)

Army Form C. 2118.

Place	Date	Hour	Summary of Events and Information	Remarks and references to Appendices
Field	6-1-18		(Backward from last pg.) which leaves (Sim) Pvt. Ames to man leave completed service on return to division in regard to guns etc. A.D.O.S XIX Corps	W
	7-1-18		Visited railway; also men & O/C Coy; stayed with the back a instructions at K.S. met: approximately a battalion of O/C a group visiting refugees tonight. Visited D.H.Q.S who arrived during the day for a long stay in present area.	
				Passed
	8-1-18		Left dist shop. Visited OUDEZEELE day. Informed O/C tankable that he would get distributed at Q2 remaining long distance that to clearing of usual DOS immediately see arrangements to fixing dump of ration (day) a little info by that with Complained to SSO about Refugee rations	Passed

Army Form C. 2118.

WAR DIARY
or
INTELLIGENCE SUMMARY.
(Erase heading not required.)

Instructions regarding War Diaries and Intelligence Summaries are contained in F. S. Regs., Part II. and the Staff Manual respectively. Title pages will be prepared in manuscript.

Place	Date	Hour	Summary of Events and Information	Remarks and references to Appendices
Field	9.7.18		A.D.O.S. X Corps called with latest tanklier (last delay 9/7) S.S.O. inspected Defects return; visited Rejecting Point & (?) defects to be remedied in future.	U
	10.7.18		Visited Army lay & wounded returns of eve this evening.	U
	11.7.18		Visited Salvage Officer & arranged various inventories given by H.Q.M.C. to forward Dump (written also to fallens also D Army S of GODEWAERSVELDE. Arranged wages from 3 ton D.A.C. would be at the disposal daily of Salvage Officer. Major H.W. Brown M.C. D.D.O.S. returned from Staff - visited Kingston.	
	12.7.18		Visited R.H.2. Reported to A.D.O.S. at Esshood. Visited A.S.O.s also X Corps ADS. X Corps left Salvage Arrangements, arranged to visit Dump withhead, etc tomorrow. Also visited this D.W.Bess 36 Div Sappers X Corps & dépôt.	(and)

A7092 Wt. W1128 9/M1293 750,000. 1/17. D. D & I. Ltd. Forms/C2118/14.

WAR DIARY
or
INTELLIGENCE SUMMARY

Army Form C. 2118.

Place	Date	Hour	Summary of Events and Information	Remarks and references to Appendices
Lud	15-9-18	—	Visited D.H.2. & discussed the salvage question with the A.A & Q.M.G & the D.A.D.O.S. He informed me he was unable to examine salvage from the Divnl. Salvage Organization. Visited A.D.O.S. & kept a dump & kept agent time to communicate with the Divnl. salvage officer. On visiting salvage Dump visited Dump at the Lucknow found about 70 items from the Divn. thus to forward on when dump was formed. Visited about 18 30 to Divn. nearest to the lines dining about 15 M.9.a.2.5. Reported situation to A.O.&D.S.	level
	16-9-18		Visited D.H.2. who gave me instructions to move depôt from P.13 to P.3, that whole depôt partially moved with the ordn. consult to request depôt at P.13. A.O.&D.S. - D.A.D.O.S. 14 Div. came to see us & issued upon exit of 33 Jordan R.B. at front (and in Delhi are P. previous to this as) I visited the empties dump to study by detail from Dist. Am. Dep. & Splemanl. dumnel	

WAR DIARY
INTELLIGENCE SUMMARY

Army Form C. 2118.

Place	Date	Hour	Summary of Events and Information	Remarks and references to Appendices
Field	16.7.18		Visited D.H.Q., also Ordnance gun Park & 2 jo special store. Visited Div. salvage dump, attending advance our work in progress. Visited 24WD 104 Infy Bde. I stain gun 18 tanks & 25 damaged by shell fire. Replacement demanded.	[illeg]
	17.7.18		No 2 Ordnance gun Park, arrived. Visited 50 B. there and with gunner to divise into R.E. dump & Ordnance matters generally. Visited draft of 5 salvage at X Corps Gp. & Div. with gunner to all Divisions D.C. 35 mi's, length on point.	[illeg]
	July 18		Visited Div. H. 2n, also Div. salvage a roller kiln. A.D.O.S & left visited dump visited gunner my store to 35 Div. thereon. Staff left salvage X Corps called upon the great ammunition [illeg]	[illeg]

Army Form C. 2118.

WAR DIARY
or
INTELLIGENCE SUMMARY.
(Erase heading not required.)

Instructions regarding War Diaries and Intelligence Summaries are contained in F. S. Regs., Part II. and the Staff Manual respectively. Title pages will be prepared in manuscript.

Place	Date	Hour	Summary of Events and Information	Remarks and references to Appendices
Field	July 20		Реманded 16 Lewis Guns to complete Guns per Regt; awaiting 482, 486/215, R.F.A. 16 & Lewis Visited Bgd H.Q. In dales delays of them with Bosnes. Visited O.C. 19 M.G. to get all salt dump. Visited O.C. 25 M.G.B. re Lewis Guns & delays of them Visited Fd Amb re Sewn Curtains & making of stretcher during re wounded gas	(cont)
	July 21		Visited D.H.Q. Demanded Lewis Guns to 18 L.F. to replace one condemned. Visited re missing of Lewis Limbers for allowed clearing of surplus R.E. dump.	(cont)
	July 22		Visited Armies. Arranged removal of Division to the whole of the Duplex R.O.F. of K.E. emm. Dead R.A.S.?	(cont)
	July 23		Returned from Abberville. Visited D.A.D.Z.R. reported progress. Thinking guns destroyed and in last complete turn out for myself demanded to complete to new	(cont)

A/092   Wt. W 1218 9/M 1293   750,000. 1/17. D.D & I. Ltd.   Forms/C2118/14.

Army Form C. 2118.

WAR DIARY
or
INTELLIGENCE SUMMARY.
(Erase heading not required.)

Place	Date	Hour	Summary of Events and Information	Remarks and references to Appendices
Field	July 24		Visited road & loop also Bn HQ's & advance dumps with P.O. 2nd My. Removed 3/E. Ready from salvage dump, visited S.C. Salvage, also S.C. 19 Inspirations, salvage office when intruded 18 PDR B/159 wire coming. Ground destroyed by shell fire	(saud)
	July 25		Visited Bn HQ, Richard, O.P.O.'s & loops, loops; visited salvage officer, also loops salvage dump. Visited HqQuarter Rifle salvage day & took this delivery over & where ever. Divided to move salvage office to point outside Boisleux, keeping dump receiving that much as main assembling was 2nd S. Confined situation & railway up recovery little wire ones leavings	(saud)
	July 26		Private Hudson, G.S.6699, howark T.L. 194050 Suffock R.A. 479960 of 232 Enp: Coy accident 3S Bull Salvage loop, wounded by steel fire & visited Bn H2n also Leaving for local purchase of Lamps for Sig: & O.P. officers	(saud)

WAR DIARY
or
INTELLIGENCE SUMMARY.

Army Form C. 2118.

Place	Date	Hour	Summary of Events and Information	Remarks and references to Appendices
Field	July 26		Visited salvage dump. Arranged with Q to send lorry to Salvia to collect drawn workshop by 106 Infy Bde. 11 Div. Tried Repair workshop.	U
	July 27		Visited B&I 2 & field. Applied to ORS for leave to authority to draw 1950 Watch Back from Ord. dep & workshop July 28-1918. Visited Repair & workshop. BABS 36 Divn withdrew reserve of clothing to Anti-Gas Divn making provisions. Divn 36 Divn also completed at army depot. vis 32 men to their units at army to defences. Demands 1-18 per men from 159 Bde to replace one (5689) sick by check from handed by 10th.	Paul
	July 28		Indent two Vickers Guns only for 15 Inf Btn to replace one damaged by shell fire. All special stores for 106 Infy Bde drawn & issued. Visited Air tb gas alarm salvage dump.	Less

Army Form C. 2118.

WAR DIARY
or
INTELLIGENCE SUMMARY.
(Erase heading not required.)

Instructions regarding War Diaries and Intelligence
Summaries are contained in F. S. Regs., Part II.
and the Staff Manual respectively. Title pages
will be prepared in manuscript.

Place	Date	Hour	Summary of Events and Information	Remarks and references to Appendices
Field	July 29	-	Visited Bn. H.Q. Went to the Orne to try trains for use. 106 Infy Bde for an urgent of special papers.	(contd)
	July 30		Visited Bn.2 who were always down. Demanded destruction for replacement of the condemned arranged with 156 Bat. R.G.A. to inspect horses were of the Brigade at 10.30am Aug. 1st.	(contd)
	July 31		Visited Bn. 2nd, where its doties Kd wire left Kurnt. arranged a map of the whole Rn. rebuilt, leaving a map for my successor Stef for this purpose. Principle issues of work done in this Army from 1.7.18 to 31.7.18	
			Machine gun train opened a sinehed	61
			" " " " "	65 / 15
			Lewis distribution	8
			Magazines " "	5 / 6
			Rifle G.S.	7
			Bayonets & scabbards	
			Pistol	121
			Steel Helmets	
			Bayonets	

WAR DIARY
INTELLIGENCE SUMMARY.
(Erase heading not required.)

Army Form C. 2118.

Place	Date	Hour	Summary of Events and Information	Remarks and references to Appendices
Field	July	—	Work done in Boot, Boot & Tailors shops for 1.7.18 to 31.7.18.	Laud
			Boots & ankle for repair issued — 206	
			" " overhauled & issued — 1,261	
			Puttees for repair — 1,199	
			L. Australian Purser	
			Major	
			D.A.D.O.S. 3rd Div.	

WAR DIARY / INTELLIGENCE SUMMARY

Army Form C. 2118.

D.A.D.O.S. 35 Division
1st – 31st August 1918

Vol 30

Place	Date	Hour	Summary of Events and Information	Remarks and references to Appendices
Field	Aug 1		Visited D.H.Q. Inspected Hammer ex. of the 157 Brigade R.F.A. with the C.O. and Baring 35 Div–Missed Duel later Killer.	haut
	Aug 2		Visited Bde 2. also Bdes 36 Bde. A.D.O.S. & Reap visited depôt & inspected lack of Brigadier & entertaining indents. Pointed out that the men were told to ever week. due not to their fault to outrunning the pushers. It 100 worth of junk. Purchased special cutting of junk as surveyed American Interventions. A.D.o.S & Reap. letter to A.D.o.S Army under	haut
	3		Visited G.H.Q. Visited Quel Salvage Officer of Ordn Stores on Salvage Dumps and gave defenite instructions all Ordn Stores are to be returned to me & Unit & must not be accepted at Salvage Dumps unless the Unit can clearly prove that they are genuine Salvage.	haut
	4		Parade for commencement of 5th year of the war. Visited D.H.Q. Visited Corps H.Q. to see A.D.O.S. & Staff Captain Salvage my return of Soldier & dead.	haut
	5		Visited D. H. Q. Visited O.C. French Mission & arranged to evacuate the furniture &c of a Refugee Family to Bavinchove.	haut

WAR DIARY
or
INTELLIGENCE SUMMARY

Army Form C. 2118.

Place	Date	Hour	Summary of Events and Information	Remarks and references to Appendices
Field	6/8/18	—	Visited @ H.Q.; Visited ADOS & Corps reference scrap & obtained authority to buy up to £100. Went to Calais with O.C Trench Mission & bought scrap. Visited 600 Calais I/h and reorganized this division's trench situation. Held musters.	Cau S
	7/8/18	—	Visited @ H.Q. - DADMG arranged with 30th Divn that in the Divl Relief Aug 8-10th my depot to remain in its present situation. Sent lorry (and Corps Coligny?) to Calais to bring back scrap. Visited Staff Captain Salvage & gave him crossbar for their Trophy Exhibition.	Cau S
	8/9/18	—	Visited @ H.Q. Arranged for Salvage C.'s to come out of the line on Aug 10th & to go to St Marie Cappelle for a rest. Soldiers lefts for 104th & 105th By 13/8/18 to be sent to my depot.	Cau S
	9/8/18	—	Visited Div HQ's; Visited Corps H.Q.; Demanded 1.18pr to replace No 116 belonging to 157 Bde condemned for inaccuracy. QMG 1/QO.1.d 5.8.1918.	Cau S
	10/8/18	—	Visited Divl HQ's; Visited HQ 35 I.G.C. Visited HQ 105 of Bde re clothing of the 15th Sherwoods. This unit complained to the C.O.'s that they were unable to get their clothing from the Ordnance. Seems odd as I have very demand made by this unit from the moment	Cau S

WAR DIARY
or
INTELLIGENCE SUMMARY
(Erase heading not required.)

Army Form C. 2118.

Place	Date	Hour	Summary of Events and Information	Remarks and references to Appendices
10/8/18 cont. Field			moment it entered the field have been met in full.	
	11/8/18	—	Visited D.H.Q.; Visited A.D.O.S Corps re clothing from Base. Visited G.O.C. 164 Inf Bde also C.O.'s 19t N.F's 18 Lanc Fus & t R.E. 55 Div on General Orders Matters. Visited 55t Salvage Co re new Establto — instructed same.	Laid P
	12/8/18	—	Visited D.H.Q.; Visited C.O. 19t D.D.L.I. re preference paint for wheels. DDOS 2d Army & instructed Deput & storehouses	Laid P
	13/8/18	—	Visited D.H.Q.; Visited Ag. Officer 2d Army H.Q. to obtain forms & noted for 35t Div. Dow Agencies Party. Visited Div Sales Station to obtain Cot St Bt Solder. Re noted D.H.Q. re complaint made by G.O.C. 35t Div direct to Corps that he was unable to obtain clothing for the R.A. of his Div. I was able to prove by my records that every demand made upon me by any R.A. unit has always been met in full.	Laid P
	14/8/18	—	Visited D.H.Q.; Visited A.D.O.S Corps reference List of Losses — went to 35t Div.; C.R.A. called re clothing — issues & demands were shown to him & it was found that statements had been made to him by Battery O.C. which did not correcte with the	Laid P

Army Form C. 2118.

WAR DIARY
or
INTELLIGENCE SUMMARY.
(Erase heading not required.)

Instructions regarding War Diaries and Intelligence Summaries are contained in F. S. Regs., Part II. and the Staff Manual respectively. Title pages will be prepared in manuscript.

Place	Date	Hour	Summary of Events and Information	Remarks and references to Appendices
Field	14/8/18 (contd.)		the facts. The D.R.A. is taking the matter up with the O.C.s concerned. Saw D.A.M.G. 10th Corps ref paint G.S. – local purchase approved up to £25. Indent for 159 demanded to replace one for ceiling.	paint
	15/8/18		Visited Q.M. H.Q. 1200 lb of paint arrived up from Base so have decided not to buy locally for the present. Started a 3rd Soldier Kehr at Sheet 27 Q 20.a.; 12 Sub Kedo for D.T.M.O arrived from Order	last Q
	16/8/18		3rd Depot Divn H.Q., visited A.D. of S. I Corps; visited Kelso; visited Kehr and Salvage Dumps	W
	17/8/18		Visited 6.0.0 Calais with D.A.A.N.G reference paint, soap, stationers questions	W
	18/8/18		visited Div H.Q. on to myself from Q.M by a sergeant of Div H.Q. on to myself from Q.M by a sergeant had been made to Div H.Q.	W
	19/8/18		visited Div H.Q.; visited 6.0 15 Cheshires and his stores; visited Salvage Coy; visited Staff Capt. 106 Bde. reference transport of the 17th Royal Scots; the ½ tonn Java for Field Coy. R.E. arrived today from the Gun Park. Decided to build a second solid Kiln at Dy depot here.	W
	20/8/18			

A7092 Wt. W1285 9/M1293 750,000. 1/17. D. D. & L. Ltd. Forms/C2118/14

Army Form C. 2118.

WAR DIARY
or
INTELLIGENCE SUMMARY.
(Erase heading not required.)

Place	Date	Hour	Summary of Events and Information	Remarks and references to Appendices
In the Field	20/8/18		Visited Div. HQrs. went into the question of average issues of clothing per 100 men with the D.A.Q.M.G. visited D.Q.M.G. reference the clothing of his men, and in G. called & inspected clothing returned to me by a unit as unserviceable & having sent a report to Div. HQrs. upon this point.	
	21/8/18		Visited Div. HQrs. memo arrived from D.O.S. 2nd Army recalling my chief clerk and sending him back to 1st Army HQrs. for duty. Saw A.A. & Q.M.G. on this point who is taking the matter up with higher authority.	W
	22/8/18		Visited Div. HQrs. train O.B. 35 M.T. Co. who want my car A. 1220 in for complete overhaul, which he estimates will take 14 days. Visited Salvage agent Entin Kilns. Trotter always 10 other reference Corps Rest Station. Saw T.O. 10th S.p. Bde. reference Backwardry and the transport of the 10th Lane Fus.	W
	23/9/18		Visited Div. HQrs. sent car 1220 to 35-M.T. Coy for overhaul. Saw A/Staff Capt. 105 Inf Bde reference the absence names of Pans & Lloyd 6 Bar R??. and asked for a report, O.B. 107 field Ambulance called reference Salvage Officer called, O.B. 107 field Ambulance called reference the clothing for Anti Mustard Gas work which was handed over to 30 Division, awarded the French Croix de Guerre	W

WAR DIARY or INTELLIGENCE SUMMARY

Army Form C. 2118

(Erase heading not required.)

Place	Date	Hour	Summary of Events and Information	Remarks and references to Appendices
	24/8/18		with étoile de bronze under a citation à l'ordre de la Division G.O. No 376 dated 17.8.18. Wave of Chief Clerk cancelled. Visited Div. Hqrs. Visited Kitchen Anneke. Stopped timbering workshop with rained timber.	W
	25/8/18		Visited Div. Hqrs. Staff Capt. 104 Inf. Bde called.	W
	26/8/18		Visited Div. Hqrs. AADVS with DDMG visited depot. Inspected new barns for troops of the — Div. Passing through.	W
			E.O. 17 [?] inn closed. AADMG with ADDVS 36th Div. called reference move. Went to see depot of AADVS 36th Div.	
	27/8/18		Visited Div. Hqrs. Visited DADVS 36th Div. to make further arrangements as to the move. Visited ADOS. Both Div.	W
	28/8/18		Visited Am Hqrs. Visited Kitchen Anneke. Visited 36. 35. M.T. Coy. Visited R.J.A. No. 3239 condemned for roaring.	W
	29/8/18		18 Para 15.7. Pte R.J.A. No. 3239 condemned for roaring. Visited Am Hqrs. Sent A/Staff Sergt Bradley to England for a three months tour of duty. Sent A/Staff Sergt to 106 Inf. Bde.	W
	30/8/18		to convalescent L. of C. bh. Jenna Curro. Visited Div. Hqrs. AA & QMG visited depot reference move. Staff Capt. Salvage 10th Corps called reference move. Staff Capt. called reference Latrine Pails for area. DADMG ADMS called reference 36th Div. called reference Anke for Clothing.	W
	31/8/18		36th Div. with DADVS. 36th Div. called reference Anke for Clothing to be handed over. Move with 36th Div. suspended.	W

Army Form C. 2118

WAR DIARY
or
INTELLIGENCE SUMMARY
(Erase heading not required.)

Place	Date	Hour	Summary of Events and Information	Remarks and references to Appendices
	3/9/18		Visited Divl. Hqrs. Brought Salvage Co. back to my Depot. Salvage for month 486 tbs.	A

L Cavalsin Nurse
Major
On O.C. 93rd Bde Rn

War Diary.

D.A.D.O.S. 35th Brit Divn

Period. Sept 1st to 30th 1918.

Volume II.

Army Form C. 2118

WAR DIARY
or
INTELLIGENCE SUMMARY
(Erase heading not required.)

No. M 31

Place	Date	Hour	Summary of Events and Information	Remarks and references to Appendices
Jn Cu	1/9/18		Visited Div Hqrs. Visited Hqrs 30th American Division reference taking over; visited A.D.O.S. 2nd Corps; also D.A.Q.M.G. 2nd Corps reference Depot in new area.	W
	2/9/18		Visited Div Hqrs. Visited Ordnance Officer 30th American Div and arranged to take over his Depot in rotation. Saw Q.O.C. and arranged for him to take over new Depot; visited A.A & Q.M.G and American and shewed him new Depot; visited A.A & Q.M.G and explained situation from Ordnance point of view.	W
	3/9/18		Visited Div Hqrs. Moved office to American Depot. Visited H.Q. 2nd Corps to arrange Salvage Questions. Holden in new area.	W
	4/9/18	—	Visited Q H.Q - Railhead Sancte - old Depot & arranged for removal of running shoes forward.	W
	5/9/18	—	Visited D.H.Q - met the new D.A.D.M.G. Lt Col Jones D.S.O. Visited Railhead; Visited A.D. and 2nd Corps reference clothing for Anti Gas purposes. Explained situation to D.A.Q.M.G. & asked Corps for immediate authority to draw 250 suits from O.O. 2nd Corps Troops. Am Corndt. Water Area called at Depot reference	W.

Army Form C. 2118.

WAR DIARY
or
INTELLIGENCE SUMMARY.
(Erase heading not required.)

Place	Date	Hour	Summary of Events and Information	Remarks and references to Appendices
Field	5/9/16 cont.		reference precautions to be taken in event of (Shelling) of the River at end of Depot becoming swollen. Salvage to moved forward to Proven + reported to Staff Capt. Salvage for Duty. (F.7. & S.4). Arranged to build two solder Kilns in centre of new Transport Area. Lce Serjeant T. ordered to report to O.O. XIth Corps Troops for duty, relief being sent to me by O.O. IInd Corps Troops. Took over Surplus stores (Petrol) from O.O. 30th American Div. giving him a receipt for same & reporting transaction to act concerned -----	W
	6/9/16		Visited D.H.Q. - Spent day in arranging Depot. workshops, Kiln &c -----	W
	7/9/16		Visited R.H.Q. saw D.A.Q.M.G. reference Packsaddlery, Solder Kilns. Lt Col Stone ADOS IInd Corps visited Depot -----	W

Army Form C. 2118.

WAR DIARY
or
INTELLIGENCE SUMMARY
(Erase heading not required.)

Place	Date	Hour	Summary of Events and Information	Remarks and references to Appendices
Field	8/9/16	—	Visited C.R.H.Q. - Railhead - Corps Salvage Dump to see Divisional Salvage Officer & to arrange for his move forward. Visited forward area to choose sites for Salvage Stores.	W
	9/9/16	—	Visited D.H.Q. - Visited A.D.O.S. 2nd Corps reference code calls for Salvage Dumps. Visited Corps Salvage & fixed to move 1st Salvage Co. at 2pm to Brandhoek G.12.d.8.6. & to Pioneer June. H.16.c. Visited CO 105 Field Ambce & arranged for him to put my men at Soldat Kuhr 28.f.11.a.9.9. Took men forward & established Soldat Kuhr. Visited OC 35 Bomb Store. Visited DADOS 4 Div. - O.O. 2nd Corps troops ref. Gas Defence in Area.	W
	10/9/16	—	Visited Divl. HQ. Visited CRA 35th Divn. Staff Capt. reference Horse Blankets for 157 Bde R.F.A. Visited ADOS 5th Corps with Capt Kinch reference Racks for packing Lewis Guns on Limbers. Gas Officer 35th Divn called reference Salvage &c Appliances from U.S.A. units. Visited I.O.M. % Mobile Workshops re Axletrees.	W

Army Form C. 2118.

WAR DIARY
or
INTELLIGENCE SUMMARY.
(Erase heading not required.)

Instructions regarding War Diaries and Intelligence Summaries are contained in F.S. Regs., Part II. and the Staff Manual respectively. Title pages will be prepared in manuscript.

Place	Date	Hour	Summary of Events and Information	Remarks and references to Appendices
Field	10 Cont		re Archives to taken over by me from 30th American Div. Visited C.O. 30th N.G. Battn. at General Ords. questions. Visited Salvage Co. at 28 G.12. totaled Kilns at 28 G.11. (Demanded) 3" Stokes Barrel for 106 MV3 - received same day.	W
	11/9/16	-	Visited O.H.Q. - C.O. 19th N.Z. - Salvage Co. - totaled other 28.9." which is now furnished & working - delivered in lots of Wood to this Kiln for working purposes. Visited Railhead	W
	12/9/18	-	Visited D.H.Q., Visited E.R.E. reference drainage of Depot. Demanded two Lewis Guns for + N.C.E. Staff to replace 2 destroyed by shell fire.	W
	13/9/16	-	Visited O.H.Q. Visited ADOS 2nd Corps reference hot food containers	W
	14/9/18	-	Visited D.H.Q. Visited ADOS 2nd Corps, also Salvage Co. totaled Kilns. Demanded 1 Lewis Guns for 15th N.Z. to replace one Gun demanded. Major Hower D.A.D.O.S completed four years unbroken service in France to day	W

WAR DIARY
or
INTELLIGENCE SUMMARY.
(Erase heading not required.)

Army Form C. 2118.

Place	Date	Hour	Summary of Events and Information	Remarks and references to Appendices
Field	15/9/18		Visited @ H.Q.; Division transferred to 19th Corps; Visited ADMS 19th Corps; spoke to him about Lot. Foot containers, racks for Lewis Guns, + socks for Duck Baths. Visited Staff Capt. Salvage 19th Corps. & gave him map locations of Dumps & Solatz Kilns (Demanded 1.4.5 How for 157 Bde on Sep 14, same released by wire today.)	Ans'd
	16/9/18		Visited @ H.Q.; Visited C.R.A. 25th Div with reference to Panniers etc. for pack vehicles. Toured area to find site for a Depôt. Demanded 200 nob Pack Saddlery, + 100 Racks for carrying Water Tins from ADOS 19th Corps.	Ans'd
	17/9/18		Visited D.H.Q. Settled for new Depôt 28.F.8.c.4.4. & started to move Stores So. Visited G.O.C. 104th Infy Brigade.	Ans'd
	18/9/18		Visited D.H.Q.; Completed move. Visited ADOS 19th Corps. (20kb) for 100 Yukon Packs also 1500 Water Bottles. Authority to draw Packsaddlery "Packs arrived, arrange to send forward for same first thing 19th D.A.Q.M.G. reaches new Depôt.	U Ans'd

Army Form C. 2118.

WAR DIARY
or
INTELLIGENCE SUMMARY.
(Erase heading not required.)

Place	Date	Hour	Summary of Events and Information	Remarks and references to Appendices
Field	19/9/18		Visited D.H.Q. & Salvage Dumps. A.D.O.S. 19 Corps called at Depot. Visited 19 Corps "Q" re reference ships for signalling. I pointed out to Corps "G" that I would make the ships up for the whole of the Corps on my Tailors shop. Authority received for 400. 19/9/18 4.20 p.m. Summoned Carried. Closed down the follow= =ing at 27½.14. & required at 28½.14. 35 D.O.S.R.A. to discuss the allotment of the special carriers for Ammn - obtained same. A.D.O.S. 19 Corps called at Depot took away the signalling ships for the Corps.	Am̅ S 1
	20/9/18			Am̅ 1
	21/9/18		Visited D.H.Q. Visited O.C. 107 Bde R.F.A. reference saddle blankets & Transit. Issued Transport Officer 100 Sft. of reference Petrol tins & jerker Packs for lever. Issued D.A.T charge to 1 Div Field Ambn. Drew 100 Guitar Packs for 100 Supplie to O.O.A.T. No. 3. Division credited with 2.2. Lg.Lbs for all Vickers Sword. Watch Car Guns.	Am̅ 1

Army Form C. 2118.

WAR DIARY
or
INTELLIGENCE SUMMARY.
(Erase heading not required.)

Place	Date	Hour	Summary of Events and Information	Remarks and references to Appendices
Field	22/9/18	-	Visited @ H.Q. Attended Parade of Pack Saddlery Troops before the G.O.C. Division. Visited D.R.A. reference to M/73 Bde R.F.A. & arranged that DADOS 36th Divn should continue to administer & issue them for Ordnance Services. Two Cos of the 101 N.F. Bank attached to this Divn for Ord.a Services from 19 Corps Troops.	(Ans)
	23/9/18	-	Visited D.H.Q. Katheads M/3 19th Corps reference L.F. Ammn Carriers, Gen R.A. Visited O.C. 135th M.G. Batts reference S.D. Clothing demanded for his Unit. Visited D.O. 19th Corps Troops & drew Vickers Guns for S.A.A. to 101 M.G.C.	(Ans)
	24/9/18	1	Visited D.H.Q. Visited the Salvage Co also forward Dumps. Arranged for all salved Deer Stewards to be sent to I.B.D. dumps at Branohock; Visited Soldrs Hrs. S.A.A. & visited Depot. Visited R.D. of 10th Corps reference stores (Ord.a) handed over by this Divn to the 30th American Divn.	(Ans)
	25/9/18	-	Visited @ H.Q. Visited O.O. Army Gun Carts No 2 for 40 Wire Gutters urgently required. O.C. No 1 Co Tram Wald would reference the	U

Army Form C. 2118.

WAR DIARY
or
INTELLIGENCE SUMMARY.
(Erase heading not required.)

Instructions regarding War Diaries and Intelligence Summaries are contained in F. S. Regs., Part II. and the Staff Manual respectively. Title pages will be prepared in manuscript.

Place	Date	Hour	Summary of Events and Information	Remarks and references to Appendices
Field	25/9/16		cont. the franking of transport on the site used by my lorries. Visited Dule Salvage & (O/C Salvage went on leave to England 24.9.16). Visited O/C R.E. reference to cave of Cycles by Scouts. Tested O.C. Signals ref special flags for runners. Demanded 3 Lewis Guns for 1/9 D.L.I. replace destroyed rifle fire. ———	W
	26/9/16		Visited Div. H.Q.Rs. The 3 Lewis Guns for 1/9 D.L.I. received. Issued to O.C. 105 F.Amb. 100 rnds S.D. for A.A. Gun. arrived. O/C. on this subject. Visited Salvage Dumps Folders below — Tracked 104 Inf. Bde reference Pack Saddlery. 16 Pr. guns & car- riage 139 R.F.A destroyed by shell fire No 2970 & 25976.	W
	27/9/16		Visited D.A.Q. — Visited Salvage Dumps & Folder Return. Visited St Omer on local purchase & also to inspect Ord. Fld. Dumps to Q.	W
	28/9/16		Depot shelled all day — two shells totally destroyed by a direct hit but as no troops were in them no casualties occurred. (Guns) Arranged to push Salvage forward as soon as tactical situation	W

Place	Date	Hour	Summary of Events and Information	Remarks and references to Appendices
Field	29/9/18 Contd		Wheelers allowed to salve wheels tires, food containers, limbers. S.A.A. equipment rifles & mechanical traded Dumdumps & C. gave them warning order to be ready to move new forward at half an hours notice. — 76 O. of C. to remove or set aside). (9.50 am.) 22357 & 7th Green 237 Employ: Co wounded by shell fire (12.15pm) admitted to 105 Field amb. Tr: 6396 15pm Qms. [Quartermaster] premature burst - replacement demanded (2.40 pm) Ex A rang up R.O. for 2 Q.T. trigger complete for 2.19"pm urgent - ranged Gun Park & had same available at our depot. 1.40 pm. CRA duty notified - issued to Woolwich 2.30 pm sent to O.O. Gun Park No 2 for 400 13pr cannisters 2.50 & 5 cannisters urgently from Gun Park (3pm) sent lorry for same. Demanded 1 No. 7 Dial Sight for 35TRA (3pm) 1.18.9cn 9.59 destroyed by shell for replacement demanded (3.5pm). 1.4.5 How. D/157 Complete equipment to replace lost in action demanded (3.15pm)	Appx

Army Form C. 2118.

WAR DIARY
or
INTELLIGENCE SUMMARY.
(Erase heading not required.)

Place	Date	Hour	Summary of Events and Information	Remarks and references to Appendices
Field	29/9/18	(3.15pm)	Received D.H.Q. – Revised Salvage C°. & gen. orders for move of Forward Dump. 28/4 to to move at 7am tomorrow 29/9 to augochs near to Fetubre Lake 28/1.21.a. & to pulse area 14.19 +	J.
		1.20/21. (5.30pm) Owing to position at Café and loss to 1.0M 1/2 Workshops to draw 180# gun + carriage + to deliver same before 9 am tomorrow to 28/H22 a.2.7. (Lorry and 6.15pm work fatigue party)			
	29/9/18		Demand for 16 pdrs for S.P.S.S.Y. cancelled S.O.M. crew repaired. Reached D.H.Q., Demanded 1.18pm gun 10/19 to replace lost & others five. Ticket forward area for ante. for ordnance. Depot etc. Received at 28/4 9.a.6.6. & arranged to move forward first thing on the 30th. Tracked all ASST Captured to ascertain any urgent needs. Reviewed Dump D.S.O. & A.D.O.S. 19 R Corps called at Depot – Visited Salvage C° in new area.	(and)
	30/9/18		Visited Dev HQrs. Move depot to 28/14 9.a.6.6. but move was badly delayed owing to Off/3La transport not having moved as yet. Woodcock	J.

Place	Date	Hour	Summary of Events and Information	Remarks and references to Appendices
Field	30/4/17	(cont)	Visited Staff Capt. R.A. Office & also Staff Capt. R.E. returning gun demands, but he was out. Visited Q. & any R. Plumber reported destroyed - usual report to DBSa for ammunition trucks OTC of NG Battys, 15 Siege Bdes, 1 Medium, Heavy seige + 1 & reserve Ordnance number. - Visited Salvage Co. - Closed down new Salvage Stn owing to move of Units. - SROS 19th Corps called at Dept re force commander of RA. Revisited Dir HQ Q.A. (6.30 pm) and asked Q to put up the following suggestion to Corps - "That two closed trucks be placed at my disposal at Railhead which will be moved to each new Railhead during the forward move - The two trucks to be used (1) For a shop for the Repair of Boots + Gaiters (2) For a shop for the repairs of Gloves. By this means I can guarantee never to have to close down my shops + will however be able to do work at a moment's notice. This which would be impossible when moving an Ordnance Depot by the means of your lorries only. Suggestion referred to ADOS 19th Corps	Capt [signature] Lieut. Col. O. & I. in C. Jn. 35

Army Form C. 2118.

WAR DIARY
or
INTELLIGENCE SUMMARY.
(Erase heading not required.)

Instructions regarding War Diaries and Intelligence Summaries are contained in F. S. Regs., Part II. and the Staff Manual respectively. Title pages will be prepared in manuscript.

Place	Date	Hour	Summary of Events and Information	Remarks and references to Appendices
			Principal items of work done in the Divisional Workshops during the Month of Sept.	
			Machine Guns Lewis repaired & overhauled = 10	
			" " Vickers " " = 3	
			Magazines Lewis Guns " " = 190	
			Rifles " " = 151	
			Bayonets & Scabbards " " = 62	
			Pistols " " = 5	
			Steel Helmets " " = 75	
			Snow Shoes " " = 6	
			Bicycles " " = 75	
			Torches Electric Hand " " = 19	
			Boilers Field Kitchens " " = 3	
			Despatch Boxes " " = 2	
			Boot & Tailors Shop. Boots pairs repaired & renewed = 272	
			Ditto " " = 309	
			The following items have been overhauled, examined, tagged & sent to Base. — Boots pairs 1983; Jackets 1815; Pants 5740; Puttees 1720; Trousers 1792; Caps 293.	

Van ... Major
Capt ...

War Diary

D.A.D.O.S. 35 British Division

Period 1st to 31st Octr 1918

Volume 2.

WAR DIARY or INTELLIGENCE SUMMARY

Ordnance 35 Division
Army Form C. 2118.

October 1918

Vol 32

Place	Date	Hour	Summary of Events and Information	Remarks and references to Appendices
Field	1/10/18		Visited D.H.Q – Visited Staff Capt R.A. and settled all questions relating to guns on demand + to Ordnance Stores on demand generally. DADOS 1st Div called at Depot reference taking over – Visited Railhead – Visited forward area to find site for advanced Depot nearer to Div Transport – Living Shops & received at Railhead Depot – Received DHQ – ADOS 19th Corps order "OM 110 DMW" called at Depot	
	2/10/18		Visited D.H.Q – Received all Staff Capt R.A. to let me have demands in at once to replace all losses of Lewis Guns + spare parts belonging to same. Went over inclosures to OO 19th Corps Troops for 200 tents & 350 French shelters for Billets for Infy 104, 105 + 106 Inf Bdes – to be sent by lorry to Bdr Comrs & from there by G/S Wagon (Six horse) to the D.A.C to lines at 28/T29.d. Plans changed at 1400 when orders were received for lorries to be all offloaded – no tents to be sent forward but all placed at my depot. At 1630 orders arrived to send 20 tents + 50 shelters to Menin Gate fixed to go forward from there by G.S. Wagons for 104 Inf Bde at 28/T29 d – Completed by 1730 by Dempsey'ally. ADOS 19th Corps called at Depot – DQMG also called – reference tentage & lorry situation for tomorrow explained Carriage	

WAR DIARY or INTELLIGENCE SUMMARY

Army Form C. 2118.

Place	Date	Hour	Summary of Events and Information	Remarks and references to Appendices
Field	2/10/18 Cont.		Carriages 16th Div. for 9159 condemned, not repairable. Replacement demanded. 1 Vickers Guns only demanded for 301 N.F. to replace one destroyed by shell fire.	
	3/10/18		Visited C.O.H.Q. Issued Vickers to 105 & 106 Inf. Bdes. Mess Cart B/159 destroyed by shell fire – replacement available OO 9 Corps Troops and advised Overcharge C & Overstorage Dumps – asked names of same & gave orders for a better work Visited to be shown at once. Visited @ H.Q. – and further tentage to 104 Inf. Bde. Visited Ordnance Rifling Point, all Units called except 104th Inf? who are on the move. Visited Staff Capt. and 104 & 105 Inf.Bde. & O.Master of the 106 Inf.Bde to urge upon them the necessity of demanding at once all Lewis Guns – spares – drums &c also all technical stores required to put their units on a fighting footing with the least possible delay. A.O.N.G. 9th Corps called at depot. Demanded 9 Lewis Guns complete for 15 Cheshires, 15 Sherwoods & Lewis Guns complete & DK Staff & Lewis Guns complete to replace lost in action.	

Army Form C. 2118.

WAR DIARY
or
INTELLIGENCE SUMMARY.
(Erase heading not required.)

Place	Date	Hour	Summary of Events and Information	Remarks and references to Appendices
Field	4/10/18	-	Lewis Guns for Units. 105 Brigade S/I arrived 1100 - Nos Bdes now complete to establishments. Visited D.H.Q. - Visited Ordnance Park - 1309 18 pdrs 139/13de RFA condemned for scarring - replacement demanded. Visited Quetalunga Dump. Received Div HQ A.O.O. of 9/12 Corps called of move HQs & return depot. I.O. 185th Inf Bde called reference his Brigade Transport. D.A.D.V.S. called reference War Bags & horses for a general issue to units whilst in present flooded area. Demanded 3 Lewis Guns complete for 9th DLI to replace lost in action. 17th Royal Irish report 19 Lewis Guns lost in action but asked me to hold up demand as unit have not the men to man the guns issued	
	5/10/18	-	Visited D.H.Q. Orders received to move Depot - news are not mentioned on account Tanks Railhead to arranged for the evacuation of all Ordnance Stores. Lewis Guns complete demand) reserved as follows - to replace lost in action 8 Lancs to, 17/R. Inns. 6. Demanded 7 Bdes for 187 to replace one condemned for scarring. Tanks Sof 106 Inf Bde reference Lewis Guns for Los Brigade. - matter to be referred to G.O.C. 106 Inf Bde	

Army Form C. 2118.

WAR DIARY
or
INTELLIGENCE SUMMARY.
(Erase heading not required.)

Instructions regarding War Diaries and Intelligence Summaries are contained in F. S. Regs., Part II. and the Staff Manual respectively. Title pages will be prepared in manuscript.

Place	Date	Hour	Summary of Events and Information	Remarks and references to Appendices
Field	6/10/16		Visited O.HQ - Moved depot to 28/4/16 a.4.9. move extremely long owing to large Salvage & returns by Units & large Dock received of Tonnage, Provo-saddlery, Yukon Packs &c; O.E 25 Regiment Camp called reference the equipping of each & their surplus. Demanded Sortend for Div: A.D.O.S. 9th Corps noted for covering authority to Base. Carriage B/161 demanded for 157 to replace 64513 condemned. Reveated D.H.Q reference new nets & telephone for same. Visited Staff Capt. 105 y. would balance for latter figures - at Rouen avail-able from Inf. to 1800 hours. Demanded 1 Lewis Gun for "D" Staffs.; 1 Officer's Rev. to replace 8215 for 157.; 1 Carriage to replace 1022 for 157.; 1 officer's to replace 6905 for 157.; 1 Carriage B/161 to replace 33118 for 157. --	
	7/10/16		Visited D.HQ - Visited sent D.Q. to unified captured drawed gun & to arrange for same to be brought down to my depot for evacuation to Base. Visited A.E. reference Tonkage - Visited G.O.C. 104 Bde reference Our rifling Tonkage for his troops. Visited Tolonge Co - Recovered Div H.Q.	
	8/10/16		Visited O.H.R.; A.D.O.S. 9th Corps called at (Dyot) Sent allowed to lost captured guns from forward area back to my depot. Visited forward area & located several German Field Guns which I claimed for this division (305T) & arranged to save as cover as possible. Demanded Further lorries for Division from Base. 13500	

Army Form C. 2118.

WAR DIARY
or
INTELLIGENCE SUMMARY.
(Erase heading not required.)

Instructions regarding War Diaries and Intelligence Summaries are contained in F. S. Regs., Part II. and the Staff Manual respectively. Title pages will be prepared in manuscript.

Place	Date	Hour	Summary of Events and Information	Remarks and references to Appendices
Field	9/10/18		Visited D.H.Q rear – Visited D.H.Q advanced. Front Officers asking German Machine Guns & rifles – also personally visited 2 German Field Guns.	
	10/10/18		Visited DHQ – Visited Staff Capt. 104 & 105 Bde's. Took forward circular re German Guns – I have now in my depot awaiting B.O Cooper-Thompson's removal to Base. 21 Field Guns, 2 Howitzers, 10 T.M's. 131 M/guns all German, majority of which have been asked for myself. Visited Corps & Corps reserve Contest Clothing. Demanded from Base 20 Blankets for men also under rest & Reserve for the Division.	
	11/10/18		Visited O.K.Q. Demanded 226 Trench Knives & Special ditto every from OC Guns Park No 2 & ambulance 136. Issued 2 more Guns build Guns making a total of 23. The Major Gen'l commanding the 35th Div. wrote the DSMG & LASC's needed my depot & inspected the Guns captured by this Divn & asked by me. Total & have ever seen visited future – 13900 approved by D.O.S. G.H.Q.	
	12/10/18		Standing cost of lorries attending it for Calais & Base to Depot Division for Division & divn. Board – Issued 76 10 to 105 [illegible] forthwith ever & others Units to send in Transport at once for these.	

Army Form C. 2118.

WAR DIARY
or
INTELLIGENCE SUMMARY.
(Erase heading not required.)

Instructions regarding War Diaries and Intelligence Summaries are contained in F. S. Regs., Part II. and the Staff Manual respectively. Title pages will be prepared in manuscript.

Place	Date	Hour	Summary of Events and Information	Remarks and references to Appendices
Field	13/10/18		Taken two more German Field Guns making a total for the Division of 25. Visited HQ; memo. red that official photographer from G.H.Q. will visit my Spot at 1000 hours tomorrow wishes to take photos of the Guns, Mortars, & M/G Guns captured by this Division 28/9/18 to date. G.S.O. 3 (I) G.H.Q. called at Depot to inspect captured Guns. Visited Div Salvage Dump.	—
	14/10/18		Visited C.R.H.Q. The official photographer arrived & took photos of captured Guns. Visited Rathouts, also Ordnance H.Q. sent lorries extra motor lorries for R.A. Units but they had moved forward before I was able to deliver. DADS called at Depot also ADOS 19th Corps. The second Blanket for Div arrived from Base.	—
	15/10/18		Visited Div HQ. Evacuated to Base from the Plancenghe Rathout the captured German Guns Do.; Tasked forward area such a view to finding a site for Div Ord Depot – going very slow slow Ford lorry with special issue of Lewis Guns arrived forward to 105 Inf. Bde. Received Div Reference Linkage.	
	16/10/18		Visited Div HQ a.m. Visited Div HQ advanced; Visited Bde 26 Q rear of the 106 & 105 Inf. Bdes. Visited HQ 35 D.A.C. all an General Ordnance gracified Received Div Ref. ref. reference move forward & was told to forecast for 24 hours pending settlement of present situation. Warned all Staff Captains to arrange to rush up to them tomorrow all Ordnance stores urgently needed by Units asking them to nominate the most convenient spot. ADOS desires Depot reference move & winter clothing	—

WAR DIARY
or
INTELLIGENCE SUMMARY.

(Erase heading not required.)

Army Form C. 2118.

Place	Date	Hour	Summary of Events and Information	Remarks and references to Appendices
Field	17/6	1	Visited D.H.Q. - Visited A.D.O.S. & Corps; Visited forward area; Happlegate R.A. & all O.Y. of Inf. units - Delivered order stores to units forward; Returned D.H.Q.; Filled 15 German M.G. Guns & 1 Anti Tank Rifle.	—
	18/6	1	Visited C.D.H.Q; started to move depot forward to approx L 20. Having all day — opened office forward at 16.30	—
	19/6	1	Visited Div. H.Q; Visited O.R. Depot; Visited forward area to find ads for new depot. Asked permission to return 2nd Blanket to Base as units are unable to carry owing to rapid move of division.	—
	20/6	1	Visited D.H.Q. Visited forward area pulled new depot & started to move forward to 29/9 35 a 6.1. ; Clear depot at Hamerling, to be cleared — arranged for trucks to move underclothing & forward to new Railhead — Balance to come by Lorry	—
	21/6	1	Visited C. H.Q; Moved office Brigade Groups to rear depot in Boeghem — reported move to all concerned. Cleared underclothing from rear depot by rail. Very heavy work for small staff & four Lorries as distance is great & roads are in a very bad state.	—
	22/6/18		Visited Div. H.Q. Rear Gun. Arranged to finally clear Hamerling by sending blanket back to Calais also heavy chaff cutter, Iron horse, jack &c. which units cannot carry owing to the rapid advance	

Army Form C. 2118.

WAR DIARY
or
INTELLIGENCE SUMMARY.
(Erase heading not required.)

Instructions regarding War Diaries and Intelligence Summaries are contained in F. S. Regs., Part II. and the Staff Manual respectively. Title pages will be prepared in manuscript.

Place	Date	Hour	Summary of Events and Information	Remarks and references to Appendices
Tulo	22/10/18		signed the enemy. Moved Salvage Coy by Lorry to 28 C 19 d and instructed O.C. to get this near dump to near Epicheled as possible. Guns having shot not as an now able to make issues of winter clothing to the troops and so reduce the enormous bulk which rapid moves have forced me to carry along. – For although I have frequent references from units forward they know only able to take away small stores I am very urgently required to complete the fighting efficiency of their units.	
	23/10/18		D.A.Q.M.G. of the Division visited Depot. Visited Div. Stores. Sent major for three of day cleaning and straightening Depot. Demanded 12 complete Lewis Guns for 15th Cheshires to replace lost in action.	
	24/10/18		Visited Div. HQrs. made final visit to near depot. Saved area parking rifles, equipment &c. Brought 200 men now at Reception Camp. Demanded 9 complete Lewis guns for Mayne R.o.b. to replace lost in action – received and issued same day.	
	25/10/18		Visited Div. HQrs. visited staff Capt. R.H. D.A.Q.M.G. matter report reference petrol line for water in forward area. Arranged for Salvage Coy to search area for same. Demanded 1 18 pdr rammer further to replace one destroyed by a train on level crossing at ALEPADEN. Demanded 2 Lewis guns for 15 Cheshires to replace losses in action. Demanded 1 Lewis gun for 17 Lancs. to replace lost in action.	
	26/10/18		Visited Div. HQrs. Arranged with Corps for the evacuation of surplus	

WAR DIARY or INTELLIGENCE SUMMARY

Army Form C. 2118.

(Erase heading not required.)

Place	Date	Hour	Summary of Events and Information	Remarks and references to Appendices
	26/9/18		Sir Ivey also packing up wheelbarrows &c. Traffic forward after and better upon new site for repair.	
	27/9/18		Visited Ord. Wksp, visited A.O.D. 19 Corps who called at my depot. Visited Staff Capt 1/Div Sup. Col. Visited CR 1 25th Divn & depot.	
	28/9/18		Visited Ord. Wksp, visited Staff Captain 105-1706 2L/B. Visited O.C. 35 Stat. Visited Recruits, visited new men and finally visited upon site for depot at 29/H.34 at O.2. Remained in water upon site AD M.S. reference bus clothing returned to Field Wksps, who are no longer able clothing carrying, owing to Ambulance Demanded 3 Lewis Guns and Spare bags continual moves. Demanded 3 Lewis Guns and Spare bags complete for 18.10 one Lns to replace 3 lost in action (see received 29.4.18)	
	29/9/18		Starter now on move to new depot back arranged to Visited Ord. Wksps. Starter now to new depot. Visited Sir Inglis. His Store have workshops on Bougham. Visited the Ordnance Depot at new 0625 inspecting same from the Ordnance found at new 0625 inspecting on 29/H.34 Leaving whole at Brimingham. Visited Ord. Wksps Heavily shelled from 02.30 hours, depot moved to 29/H.34 Leaving whole at Brimingham	
	30/10/18		Visited Ord. Wksps. Visited Ord. Salvage Co. Visited U.C. 35-106 reference Camp reference clothing and equipping men from Reception Camp hospital	

Army Form C. 2118.

WAR DIARY
or
INTELLIGENCE SUMMARY.
(Erase heading not required.)

Instructions regarding War Diaries and Intelligence Summaries are contained in F.S. Regs., Part II. and the Staff Manual respectively. Title pages will be prepared in manuscript.

Place	Date	Hour	Summary of Events and Information	Remarks and references to Appendices
			The following are the principal items of work performed in my shop during the month of October 1918.	
			Machine gun Vickers returned & overhauled — 2 Bayonets & Scabbards 182	
			do do Lewis do do 79 SAA Pouches 206	
			Magazines Lewis Gun do do 323 Primus Stoves 8	
			Rifles 204 Bicycles 92	
			Pistols 16 Torches Electric hand 27	5
			Tailors Shop	
			Overhauled and examined 800 pairs of puttees and at Stores 153 Prs have been returned.	
			Shoemakers Shop	
			Repaired nyp returned 136 pairs of Boots. Sorted & overhauled and sent to Stores 2938 pairs unserviceable.	

L Anderson Lieut.

War Diary.
D.A.D.O.S. 35 British Divn.
Period Nov: 1st to 30th 1918.
Volume 2.

WAR DIARY
or
INTELLIGENCE SUMMARY
(Erase heading not required.)

Army Form C. 2118.

Vol 3

Place	Date	Hour	Summary of Events and Information	Remarks and references to Appendices
			November 1918	
	1/11/18	—	Visited Div. Hqrs. DADOS M.G. of Div. visited Depot. 1200 rations petrol tins arrived at my depot for water services — these have been ordered by my return order Div 2 Relief. My depot not to move. Demanded one Vickers Gun for 35 M.G. Bn. to replace one destroyed by shell fire. Demanded 1 18pdr carriage for 159 Bde R.F.A. to replace 1 condemned by D.A.K.	W
	2/11/18		Visited Div. Hqrs. ADOS 19 Corps and DDOS 2nd Army visited Depot. Moved workshop up to present Depot. Demanded 1 Vickers Gun for 35. M.G.C. to replace 1 condemned in DADOS Army Shops. Visited Div. Salvage Dumps and instructed him to look out at once for forward right for dumps and for Solown Kiln. Two 18pdr carriages 30691 and 46078 of Trifles Div Hqrs. Bdes condemned — replacement demanded. 1 18pdr carriage 15-g Bde condemned — replacement demanded. 14913 of 159 Bde condemned — replacement demanded.	W
	3/11/18		1 18pdr 65309 of 159 Bde condemned for serving — replacement demanded. 1 Vickers Gun 17 Regt fools destroyed by shell fire. 1 18pdr carriage 42096 of 159 Bde demanded. 1 Klumachnak 1 18pdr carriage 42096 of 159 Bde replacement — replacement demanded. 1 18pdr Gun 15.20 of condemned — replacement demanded.	W

WAR DIARY
or
INTELLIGENCE SUMMARY.

(Erase heading not required.)

Army Form C. 2118.

Place	Date	Hour	Summary of Events and Information	Remarks and references to Appendices
	4/11/18		of 157 Bde condemned for scrap - replacement demanded. Visited ADOS 10th Corps re firing area stores. Visited Div Hqrs, visited Div Reception Camp, visited Div Salvage dumps. Visited Staff Capt 105 Bde re firing in batter stores now available for return to Ordnance. ADOS 19 Corps visited depot and gave ODOS orders for Sub Comdr Zysnick to report for duty with ADOS. Demanded a few guns with tripods for 17 Royal Scots to replace other lost in action — these were lost they think in an advance and will be recovered by salvage when it is possible to search the open ground. 5 Lewis guns with tripods for 17 R. in lieu to replace losses in action. Visited Div Hqrs. Visited DAPM.	U
	5/11/18		Visited Div Hqrs. Visited forward area with Salvage Officer to select suitable forward site for salvage. Revisited situation to Q. and it was decided too few to Q. and it was decided too few to go to my own depot. Demanded 1 Thompson keep asking boy man to replace one destroyed by hostile guns fire 365 M.G. 16.	U
	6/11/18		Visited Div Hqrs. Visited ADOS 19 Corps re reference returns by ordnance which include 2 G.S. Limbers complete and 2 Lewis guns which incur 2 G.S. Limbers complete and 2 Lewis guns — after referring matter back to Army Hqs. it was decided same re limbers to go to Base and L.Ms.	U

WAR DIARY or INTELLIGENCE SUMMARY

Army Form C. 2118.

Place	Date	Hour	Summary of Events and Information	Remarks and references to Appendices
	6/4/18		continued to Gun Park.	
	7/4/18		Visited Div Hqrs (which took me 4½ hours as roads and traffic was so bad) visited Div Salvage dumps	U
	8/4/18		Visited Div Hqrs. Col. Gunn Sedgwick left for G.H.Q.	
	9/4/18		Visited Div Hqrs. Visited forward area (with great difficulty) owing to traffic to find site for new depot settled on Siegen	U
	10/4/18		Shed 29/P.12. Demanded 14·5 guns for 15 T. reserve with visited Div Hqrs. Moved to new depot and had a hard difficult day on 6 traffic on road — was unable to do enough depots owing to large numbers of wagons only to went to meet Div Hqrs to send Service worry.	U
	11/4/18		Was unable to meet Div Hqrs. to send 1800 before two visited rear depot and sent for messages salvage.	U
	12/4/18		Visited Div Hqrs. sent 6 extra lorries to clear the depot before they arrived was able to bring all forward but before they arrived I sent a warning order to be prepared to move again on 13th as shot prominence to keep lorries in readiness to act for night. No strict have called wanted to fall of fair traffic conditions this makes a most week distance and traffic	U

Army Form C. 2118.

WAR DIARY
or
INTELLIGENCE SUMMARY.
(Erase heading not required.)

Instructions regarding War Diaries and Intelligence Summaries are contained in F. S. Regs., Part II. and the Staff Manual respectively. Title pages will be prepared in manuscript.

Place	Date	Hour	Summary of Events and Information	Remarks and references to Appendices
	12/1/18		Continued evacuation but cant ob. as tell bridge over river will take some 4.5 hrs. guns for 85.7 inner.	
	13/1/18		Visited Divn. Visited new area but found no accommodation at all owing to congestion of type troops. AARMG arranged to have area cleared by tomorrow. Went forward with our new O.O. only 6 fit but buildings scarcer – found 8, 100's 52 filled out – the other 300 in number having been evacuated. By the twenty Bn. left 550 lots. Visited Divn. Hqrs.	U
	14/1/18		66 Reception Camp. Equipping of Austrian book and clothing with him they are asking favourers I had returned the remarks Panvene General order in question. Visited ADOS 19 Corps. R.A. 57th Bn. Visited three ERE 19 Divn.	U
	15/1/18		Visited Divn. Hqrs and located our new depot. Visited Divn. Hqrs. Visited ADOS 19 Corps. Visited O.C. 35 M.G. Bn. & 12 Lorries ADOS 19 Corps lorries for new arrangement through DRMG to move ac groups which have to move depot at Inti.	U
	16/1/18		Thuluche area (sheet 29 H 11 to A. 6) Depot cleared by 08.50 hours. Visited Div. Hqrs and reported.	U

Army Form C. 2118.

WAR DIARY
or
INTELLIGENCE SUMMARY.
(Erase heading not required.)

Instructions regarding War Diaries and Intelligence Summaries are contained in F. S. Regs., Part II. and the Staff Manual respectively. Title pages will be prepared in manuscript.

Place	Date	Hour	Summary of Events and Information	Remarks and references to Appendices
	17/11/18	Continued	reported to gun shops re establishing new depot for 12.15 hours. A record move for this detachment.	A
	18/11/18		Moved office to Thenelbeke. Visited On. Hgrs. of G.H.Q. Visited new depot ADOS 19 Corps called at depot. Reference clothing. Int. Wright Pioneers - also for stables & prisoners. Also reference to the equipping of prisoners re the educational schemes. Visited Div. baths and inspected stock of clothing.	A
	19/11/18		Visited Div. Hqrs. (Arec) Moved salvage B. G. back to Visited Faithurst.	A
	20/11/18		Visited On. Hqrs. DAQ MG called at Depot. There were demobilisation orders attached thereto - no detail orders yet received. Visited 26 Div. Reception Camp, reference any ordnance equipment given to fallen Pioneers of same as seen issued by the Division.	A
	21/11/18		Visited On. Hqrs. Visited Staff Capt. 35 Div. R.A. reference demobilisation of the guns attached to this division. Visited 2 Lbs. of R.E. boy 2 st. train in general ordnance matters. Visited Staff Capt. 104. 105 A	A
	22/11/18		in general ordnance matters. Visited Div. Hqrs. Visited ADOS 19 Corps. reference evacuation to	

Place	Date	Hour	Summary of Events and Information	Remarks and references to Appendices
	22/1/18 continued		Base therefore rather crowded & temporary closed owing to congestion at the Base. Received warning move order for the Divnny appears likely to mean much of travel making tough. Officers kits only to be reduced that coys and men going for the while taken for 35 miles train. reference to thands for working parties largely in excess of scale - made reference to H.Q. for ruling. Figures given and also Staff Capt. C.T. reference there so far the Base to commandeer rendering available for duty another 6 officers to be sent down. Govt. timber. 6 very thick logs by 14 by R.X. in future purchase have been cut and sawn in to have & all ordnance returnees and not for re-issue & and require to be checked — this was neither 20-Div Salvage Co and supply to same seems all devoid of carriage owing of failure of the assistant MT. much depend of the enemy from the better methods for the fighting strong back of there. Unit. write to the GOCR enquiry for the return of "I" with Corps Reinforcements to the unit.	V
	23/1/18		Visited (a) KOO, (b) roads (Rochead); Visited (c) Ordce 5th Army. Verbal of Ord referred trading of O9166 Private Thompson H06 to this Unit from Calais Base. Visited O.C 106 Field Amb. re General Ordnance matters. 4.5" Hows demanded (20 × 16) to replace No. 2099 condemned for	V

Army Form C. 2118.

WAR DIARY
or
INTELLIGENCE SUMMARY.
(Erase heading not required.)

Instructions regarding War Diaries and Intelligence Summaries are contained in F. S. Regs., Part II. and the Staff Manual respectively. Title pages will be prepared in manuscript.

Place	Date	Hour	Summary of Events and Information	Remarks and references to Appendices
Field	24/11/18		Forwarded by S.O.M. D.O. W/r O.M. W.	
	25/11/18		Visited Q. Hd.; Visited Hd. Harges re return of Harness Saddlery to me by disbanded R.A. units (attached). Throughout D.H.Q. for salvage &c to move to new area by rail on 28/11/18. Arranged further for 31 trucks to be at my disposal on 28th to move my workshops, running S.O. to new area.	U
	26th		Visited Hd. Q. Left in car at 10.00 hours to billet in new area – arrived at 16.10 & did billeting.	U
	27th		During to breakdown of Car spent night in roadside. Arrived back at O.H.Q at 16.00 hours.	U
	28th		Visited D.H.Q.; sent all shops &c to new area by rail. Two Lewis Guns complete demanded (27th) for the Lane Lewis to replace lost in action.	U
	29th		Moved Offices &c to new area Sholeques. – move completed by 17 hours. Visited D.H.Q en route	U

Army Form C. 2118.

WAR DIARY
or
INTELLIGENCE SUMMARY.
(Erase heading not required.)

Instructions regarding War Diaries and Intelligence Summaries are contained in F. S. Regs., Part II. and the Staff Manual respectively. Title pages will be prepared in manuscript.

Place	Date	Hour	Summary of Events and Information	Remarks and references to Appendices
Field	30/1		Tested Sh Omer I met O.A.P.M.G.	
			Principle items of work performed in my Shops during Month of Nov.	
			Armourers Shop.	
			Guns Vickers repaired & overhauled --- 4	
			„ Lewis „ „ --- 19	
			Rifles „ „ --- 39	
			Bayonets „ „ --- 69	
			Magazines Lewis Guns --- 49.	
			Hot Hebrits --- 112	
			Bicycles --- 107	
			Inches Electric --- 8	
			Pistols --- 6	
			Stationary Boxes --- 4	
			Horse Clowers --- 8	
			Boot Shop. 1368 pairs overhauled of which 233 pairs have been re-	W
			paired & received & 1135 yet hogged & sent to Base	
				L Marshall Major
				Major RAOC
				DADOS 35 Pod Div

War Diary.
—
G.S.(?).
—
35th Bril Divsn.
—
Period. Dec: 1st to 31st 1918.
—
Volume 2.

H.Q.
35TH DIVISION
(GENERAL STAFF).
No. GA 2243
Date 14.1.19

Army Form C. 2118.

H.Q.
35TH DIVISION
(GENERAL STAFF).
No. GA 1273
Date 11/4/19

WAR DIARY
or
INTELLIGENCE SUMMARY.
(Erase heading not required.)

Instructions regarding War Diaries and Intelligence Summaries are contained in F. S. Regs. Part II. and the Staff Manual respectively. Title pages will be prepared in manuscript.

Place	Date	Hour	Summary of Events and Information	Remarks and references to Appendices
Field	1/3	—	Worked D.H.Q. & sent D.A.Q.M.G. to Doghead move to Tilques asked for 6 Motor Lorries to form Depot.	ʊ
	2/3	—	Visited Tilques & selected Depot. A 35 commence move to new area.	ʊ
	3/3	—	Arranged details with ADS & G & bops re administration of Lorban moving 65 Labor Group. Rear Divisions have DADMG hard at work checking indents & employed the whole day in checking indents sent in by Supp Demands on Base & reported progress to Q Branch 11/2 Corps	ʊ
	4/3	—	Moved to new area Tilques. Arranged to rept to D.H.Q. by car. Issued orders to DAOMG 19th Corps re bookg re taken over issued e.o.te Lakat to convey all stores for new units to D.H.Q. Nauroy &c	ʊ
	5/3	—	Visited Railhead & D.H.Q.	ʊ
	6/3	—	ADOS 19th Corps called re 65 Labour Group - explained scheme	ʊ
	7/3	—	Arranged with ADS to take job title to rept L/I Units at Nauroy Divs S Reserve Stores for Depot. DAOMG 35 Div commenced new stock	ʊ

D. D. & L., London, E.C.
(10541) Wt W8500/P713 750,000 3/18 E 2688 Forms C/2118/11.

Army Form C. 2118.

WAR DIARY
or
INTELLIGENCE SUMMARY.
(Erase heading not required.)

Instructions regarding War Diaries and Intelligence Summaries are contained in F. S. Regs., Part II. and the Staff Manual respectively. Title pages will be prepared in manuscript.

Place	Date	Hour	Summary of Events and Information	Remarks and references to Appendices
Field	7th cont		Sent this formation to DDVO giving lists of Medium HDs.	S
	8th		ADVC today stated that thin Clothing for Units of bn later Group, in addition to Turnshoes, should be QD. I was met a lorry to administer the story pending first arrangement to Units to Army HQ.	S
	9th		Took ADOS to Stores re special equipment for Educational Purposes. 2 Lewis Guns for Instant Inn. riverwagons Nos Don Park.	S
	10th		Visited HQ + got 9 Books to look who know those + Ord. Inspectors generally. Reportsorded to A. + SH Divn.	S
	11th		Nil	S
	12th		Yesterday ind. to see DAQMG on various Ordnance matters. Spoke to OO Field Stores Calais re delay in delivery of Horse Rugs and Boots Blankets. These are to be put on rail at once.	S
	13th		Inspected Part-Clothing of mk AlK Staff. Assemgd for inspection.	S

D. D. & L., London, E.C.

WAR DIARY
or
INTELLIGENCE SUMMARY.
(Erase heading not required.)

Army Form C. 2118.

Place	Date	Hour	Summary of Events and Information	Remarks and references to Appendices
Field	13/7/15 Cont		of remainder of Bat⁺ on Sunday. D.A.Q.M.G. called re complts, blk. too.	U
	14/7/15		Issued clothing to 1st Cheshire Regt. Carriage aprls⁺ of R.O. Clothing required 1,000 Horse Rugs & 2,000 Blankets asked from Base in response to rarage of regt.	U
	15/7/15		Delivered 1000 Horse Rugs & 2000 Blankets to Units.	U
	16/7/15		Inspected Clothing of 1st Norf. Deft. Approx 250 suits required to replace fair wear & tear. Demanded 16 prs. carriages for 15 & 16 Batty 15 Bde R.F.A. (Each) to replace condemnation by S.A.O.	U
	17/7/15		Completed inspection of Clothing of N. Staffs approx 250 suits reqd any to replace fair wear & tear. Clothing on change of this Unit will looked after equally as regards pairs by made tailor. Demanded & Traurge (Q.F. 18 pdr) for B/157, 15 Bde R.F.A. to replace Carriage condemned by I.O.M. O.C. 3 Soldier on horge) access issued of S.D. clothing to 1st Cheshire & 1st Renards, & N. Staffs as result of inspections.	U

Army Form C. 2118.

WAR DIARY
or
INTELLIGENCE SUMMARY.
(Erase heading not required.)

Place	Date	Hour	Summary of Events and Information	Remarks and references to Appendices
Field	19/11	1	Inspected Clothing of 9/57 Bde R.F.A, 35 D.U.G signal Co. + M.M.P.	U
	20/11		Major Thomas M.C. Dads. returned off leave	U
	21/11		Visited Q.H.Q. Hosted 19th Corps H.Q. to run off D.D.F. & A.A.A.M.G. reference Tables & Forms. Tested 60 y.F.D.C.S reference Sen. Matters.	
	22		Visited G.H.Q.; Visited Staff Captains on Brigades reference General Ordnance Matters	U
	23		Visited D.D.Q's Visited D.I.C reference clues for completion of kits in my apot. Visited D.A.D.Q. Corps Comm ee on General Ordnance Matters. Arranged to lend cars to Corps Cashiers on Tuesdays in each week. Took over from 19 th Corps the following units for Administration for Ordnance Services:— Dets. 357 E.M.Co. 233 10 of War Co. 311 do 119 Sanitary Section Inland Water Transport Section	
	24		Visited D.H.O. Visited O.C. 107 Field Ambce also O.C. 35 M.T.Co. on the subject of excess issues of Clothing. Closed Depot at noon	U

Army Form C. 2118.

WAR DIARY
or
INTELLIGENCE SUMMARY.
(Erase heading not required.)

Instructions regarding War Diaries and Intelligence Summaries are contained in F. S. Regs., Part II. and the Staff Manual respectively. Title pages will be prepared in manuscript.

Place	Date	Hour	Summary of Events and Information	Remarks and references to Appendices
Field	27/5		Worked @ H.Q., Visited 600 Salar reference Book for Division. Visited AA + QMG 35 Div reference RAOC establishment with a Division	U
	30/5		GOCRA visited depot reference the Education Scheme Demanded carriage 16 fort for 13/5/19 to replace fair wear + tear. Principal items of Work performed in Workshops during month	U
			Bootshop — Overhauled + examined 889 pairs boots of which 397 pairs were repaired + returned + reissued the balance w/s being returned to Base.	
			Armourers Shop —	
			Bicycles repaired + overhauled = 59 Fire Buckets made = 24	
			Rifles " " = 55 Stationery Boxes repaired = 1	
			Steel Helmets " " = 117 Servant Clipping Mc do = 1	
			Horses Armour " " = 5 Balances Spring 100lb do = 1	
			Pistols " " = 30	
			Torches Elec " " = 5	

Laws Power
Major
DADOS
35th Brit Divn

War Diary

DADOS 35th British Divn.

Period 1st to 31st Janʳ 1919.

Volume 2.

H.Q.
35TH DIVISION
(GENERAL STAFF).
No. G.124/4
Date 5/2/19

Army Form C. 2118.

WAR DIARY
or
INTELLIGENCE SUMMARY.
(Erase heading not required.)

Vol 35

Place	Date	Hour	Summary of Events and Information	Remarks and references to Appendices
Giza	1/9		Visited D.H.Q. Visited Area Command. Enquired reference this tour of Major Stone J.C. Told him the A.D. of the G.M.S. Train was on general interest.	W
	2/9		Visited D.H.Q. received question of Boats on River & asked for them now for my November trip. Saw authority from 165 Supt. R.Mo. on temporary terms. Looked at Road also 60 & thereto.	W
	3/9		Saw D.D.O. car out of action — had try yesterday to looked for Boats — down to shore out of use for freight carriage of Boots. Battrer.	W
	4/9	1	Visited O.H.R. discussed question of tow others Ru- on sible, Command to break out Engineer business & one and as soon as possible (See Copy orders) Told O.O. gpt up No 5 Battn & to hand over the whole of the Assistant Broyt to him.	W

WAR DIARY
or
INTELLIGENCE SUMMARY.
(Erase heading not required.)

Army Form C. 2118.

Place	Date	Hour	Summary of Events and Information	Remarks and references to Appendices
Field	5/9	—	Visited Q.H.Q. discussed War Precaution Scheme	A
	6/9	—	Visited Q.H.Q.; Visited A.D.S. of 96 Corps on General Orders Matters	A
	7/9	—	Visited D.H.Q.; Visited O.C. No 7 of War Cemetery administration. This Unit for Ordnance Stores.	A
	8/9	—	Visited D.H.Q., Visited G.O.C. 106 y 104 on Earl Order questions. Chief points raised being shortage of Boots & delay in supply of table forms.	A
	9/9	"	Visited Div. H.Q.; Sent car to G.O.C. 104 to proceed to Boulogne.	A
	10/9	"	Visited D.H.Q., Visited 12.00 K. Omer Visited DADOS 2nd Div intensive administration of local events.	A
	11/9		Visited Q.H.Q. daily. No Special items of interest to report.	A

WAR DIARY
or
INTELLIGENCE SUMMARY.
(Erase heading not required.)

Army Form C. 2118.

Instructions regarding War Diaries and Intelligence Summaries are contained in F. S. Regs., Part II. and the Staff Manual respectively. Title pages will be prepared in manuscript.

Place	Date	Hour	Summary of Events and Information	Remarks and references to Appendices
Field	16/9		Visited O HQ, Visited CO 15 Cheshires, Visited Staff Captain RA regarding clothing + excess demands. Visited DAD Stores referring loss of petrol in transit from trans	U
	17/9		Visited DAD, Capt Hardy, SA Defence Force arrived for instruction as to Ordnance Methods in the Field. Visited Rds 104+106 regarding Bivets	U
	18/9		Visited DHQ, Visited DADOS at Divs, GSO+DAQMG visited Depot, Visited 06 2nd Corps returning somewhere to be left behind – reported position to about if Corps – met Lofs to take all forward to Boulogne	U
	19/9		Visited DHQ also OC 15/Royal W. Co.	U
	20/9		Visited DHQ about DADOS, inspected clothing of B&E 157 for excess clothing. Lt Marshall Private Joy Demands?	U

WAR DIARY
or
INTELLIGENCE SUMMARY

Army Form C. 2118.

Place	Date	Hour	Summary of Events and Information	Remarks and references to Appendices
Field	21/9	—	Visited D.H.Q. — Sent car to M.T.C. for overhaul	A
	21/23	—	No law as only local Dépôt work until possible thaw to D.S.t. Advt. of troops total shortage of workable situation at our disposal none being available at Latour. A.T. [?] our own lorry from parties etc to the Dominion store	U
	24	—	Phone D.S.Q. or phone on [?] R. [?] greyhound	U
	25	—	D.D.S. + Army visited + inspected A.D.S.Y. Inspection of all heard that in 104 Fighter Capital — another excellent visit is largely due to be careful way in which they have been served	U
	26/9	—	Visited G.P.C. on Supply Sdn.	U
	27/9	—	Wrote to D.S.D. refusing work of also about Tables + forms ASC took DAQMG when we were to Dyot — car pld in W.T.C. not proteged	U

D. D. & L., London, E.C.
(13340) Wt W3500/P713 750,000 5/18 E 2688 Forms/C2118/K

WAR DIARY
or
INTELLIGENCE SUMMARY.
(Erase heading not required.)

Army Form C. 2118.

Place	Date	Hour	Summary of Events and Information	Remarks and references to Appendices
Field	28/9		Visited D.H.Q. & sent off 9/3/ph back to units of 105 Suff.3 D. as a temporary measure	W
	29/9		Called up to O.H.Q. at 2.30 a.m. Divisions moving to Calais as a temporary measure. See R.A. at 75, Field Co & 10) Field amb & Ordnance Detachment to remain at Talgues pending a solution of the situation. Visited 100 & 9th Corps as to the advisability of sending bread to Calais for stock - foot & gundery being urgently needed - decided to hold for 48 hours.	W
	30/9		Visited D.H.Q. no outside news in the Calais windows. Closed down depot for the afternoon	W
	31/9		Visited D.H.Q. Visited ADOS 9th Corps or Drocourt(?)	W

Army Form C. 2118.

WAR DIARY
or
INTELLIGENCE SUMMARY.
(Erase heading not required.)

Place	Date	Hour	Summary of Events and Information	Remarks and references to Appendices
Lille			Principle items of Work performed in my shops during the Month. —	✓
			Armourers Shop. —	
			Arms Issued Repaired = 38 ; Horse Pinned Repaired = 7	
			at Overhauled = 140 ; Bayonet Scab. Hauled = 38	
			Bicycles Repaired = 32 ; Heads Swivel Applying J. 6	
			Rifles 161 ; Misc Repaired = 1	
			as Frotas Etc. repaired 1	
			Boot Shop —	
			No. of Boots Overhauled & Examined = 2450 pairs of which 497 pairs have been repaired. Reissued to the balance bagged & sent to Base as lits.	

L Anselm Shaver
Major
ADOS 35th Divn.

WAR DIARY
or
INTELLIGENCE SUMMARY.
(Erase heading not required.)

Army Form C. 2118.

DADOS 9/9/36

Instructions regarding War Diaries and Intelligence Summaries are contained in F.S. Regs., Part II. and the Staff Manual respectively. Title pages will be prepared in manuscript.

Place	Date	Hour	Summary of Events and Information	Remarks and references to Appendices
Silgnes	1.2.19	✓	Visited Div H.Q at Calais. Saw Major General commanding. Visited C.M.D. Calais & obtained special authority for the issue of 8,000 Blankets and 150 Brasiers for use of Troops in Calais Camps. Visited Div H.Qrs at Etaples on my way back to Silgnes.	✓
Silgnes	2.2.19	✓	Visited Div H.Qrs at Etaples. Visited A.D.O.S. at Corps reference demobilization &c	✓
Silgnes	3.2.19	✓	Visited Div H.Qrs & visited O.C. R.A.F. Machine Gun Batt. reference ordnance services for this unit	✓
Silgnes	4.2.19	✓	Visited Div H.Qrs & visited Wattonceux with D.A.Q.M.G. to find site for packing & rehicle under the Cadre system.	✓
Silgnes	5.2.19	✓	Visited Div H.Qrs. Sent special Lorry to C.M.D Calais to draw Boots & gumboots. Visited C.R.A 30th Division reference Boots & Brooms explained situation to him.	✓
Silgnes	6.2.19	✓	Visited Div H.Qrs. Reported to Q. situation reference Huts drawn from C.R.E. Obtained authority for 3 extra large felt Huts for my S.C.S. Q. Reporter 1 officer & 40 O.R running to serve under my command as a special Salvage Section under the demobilization scheme	✓
Silgnes	7.2.19	✓	Visited Div H.Qrs. Etrebagnes. Visited with D.A.Q.M.G. the G.H.Q.'s 104 & V105 Inf. Brigades, also C.M.D Calais Base or general Ordnance Questions. Started building the F.C. Nation at Silgnes to deal with demobilization	✓

D. D. & L., London, E.C.

Army Form C. 2118.

WAR DIARY
or
INTELLIGENCE SUMMARY.

(Erase heading not required.)

Instructions regarding War Diaries and Intelligence Summaries are contained in F. S. Regs., Part II and the Staff Manual respectively. Title pages will be prepared in manuscript.

Place	Date	Hour	Summary of Events and Information	Remarks and references to Appendices
Tulgnes	8.2.19		Visited Div Hqrs. Obtained sanction to cancel all outstanding demands of Table V forms from them.	App 1
Tulgnes	9.2.19		Visited Div Hqrs. Total men reported from Div Hqrs. to replace men demobilized	App 2
Tulgnes	10.2.19		Visited Div Hqrs. Ascertained that G.O.C. appointed by 35" Division have been duly slacked in Chief of the Edinburgh War Museum by Q. 35" Division under instructions of G.O.C. 35" Division. Q going into necessary data as to guns handed, date of capture, state of disposal.	App 3
Hilgnes	11.2.19		To Base Truck N° V Broghill N° from my records	App 4
Tulgnes			Visited Div Hqrs V Area Commandant. Matter reference dumps left behind by D.A.D.O.S. 49" Div. Reported situation to A.D.O.S. 19" Corps.	
Tulgnes	12.2.19		Visited Div. Hqrs V also Calais Base. Visited Hqrs 104" V 105" 7th of Brigades.	App 5
Tulgnes	13.2.19		Visited Div Hqrs	App 6
Tulgnes	14.2.19		Visited Div. Hqrs	
Tulgnes	15.2.19		Visited Div Hqrs V A.D.O.S. 19" Corps on general advance questions together with Demob.	App 7
Tulgnes	16.2.19		Visited Div Hqrs V Animal Staying Camp to see of all moulds from an advance point of view	App 8

Army Form C. 2118.

WAR DIARY
or
INTELLIGENCE SUMMARY.
(Erase heading not required.)

Instructions regarding War Diaries and Intelligence Summaries are contained in F. S. Regs., Part II. and the Staff Manual respectively. Title pages will be prepared in manuscript.

Place	Date	Hour	Summary of Events and Information	Remarks and references to Appendices
Tilques	17.2.19		Visited Div Hqrs. & A.D.O.S. 19th Corps Hqrs. Visited Capt. 157 Bde R.F.A. on general ordnance matters	W
Tilques	18.2.19		Visited Div. Hqrs. The 40 men for Salvage Company reported for duty. 10 from 19th N.F. 10 from 35th M.G.C. & 20 from 18th N.Z.F.	W
Tilques	19.2.19		Visited Div Hqrs & Hqrs. 104th & 105th Inf Brigades on general ordnance matters and demobilization generally	W
Tilques	20.2.19		Visited Div. Hqrs. Visited O.C. 157 Brigade R.F.A. & the Horse Staging Camp at Esquelbecque & the stores still required to complete same. Reported situation to A.D.O.S. 19th Corps. Visited the R.N.F. M.G. Battn. & the 19th Corps about reference the returning of ordnance stores & ammunition prior to their being broken up.	W
Tilques	21.2.19		Visited Div. Hqrs. Long conference with A.D.O.S. 19th Corps on the demobilization of Locality	W
Tilques	22.2.19		Visited Div Hqrs. Visited C.O. R.N.F. Machine Gun Battn. reference the disposal of the A.A. of his unit.	W
Tilques	23.2.19		Visited Div Hqrs. Visited Area Commdt Watten & arranged to remove stores of the L.G. Dawson Tanner	W

Army Form C. 2118.

WAR DIARY
or
INTELLIGENCE SUMMARY.

(Erase heading not required.)

Instructions regarding War Diaries and Intelligence Summaries are contained in F.S. Regs., Part II. and the Staff Manual respectively. Title pages will be prepared in manuscript.

Place	Date	Hour	Summary of Events and Information	Remarks and references to Appendices
Tilques	24.2.19	-	Visited Div. Hqrs. Started taking in stores of 19th Coy. attached 4 Hunt Advance from 19th M.T. reported for duty.	US
Tilques	25.2.19	-	Visited Div. Hqrs. Visited O.C. 106th F.A. Brigade also C.O's 12th & 18th A.F.A.	US
Tilques	26.2.19	-	Visited Div. Hqrs. Visited Staff Captain 104th & 105th Inf Brigades on general ordnance questions. Gave instructions for the handing in of available stores at once	US
Tilques	27.2.19	-	Visited Div. Hqrs. Visited C.O. 159 Brigade R.F.A. & O.C's Nos 1, 3, & 4 Coys. Div. Train on demobilisation questions	US
Tilques	28.2.19	-	Visited Div. Hqrs. & 105th Fd Ambulance reference the Transport of the M.S.	US

Army Form C. 2118.

WAR DIARY
or
INTELLIGENCE SUMMARY.
(Erase heading not required.)

Instructions regarding War Diaries and Intelligence Summaries are contained in F. S. Regs., Part II. and the Staff Manual respectively. Title pages will be prepared in manuscript.

Place	Date	Hour	Summary of Events and Information	Remarks and references to Appendices
Tilques	1		Principal items of work performed in the workshops during the month of February:-	
			Guns, Lewis, repaired & overhauled ---------- 48	
			" Vickers " " ---------- 1	
			Bicycles " " ---------- 26	
			Rifles " " ---------- 28	
			Stoves, Primus " " ---------- 4	
			Bayonets & Scabbards " " ---------- 23	
			Boot Shop :-	
			150 pairs of boots repaired and re-issued.	

L Austin Shiner
Major

D.A.D.O.S. 35TH DIVISION

WAR DIARY.
DADOS. 35TH DIVISION.

For Period,

March 1st to 31st 1919.

Volume 2.

Army Form C. 2118.

WAR DIARY
or
INTELLIGENCE SUMMARY.
(Erase heading not required.)

Vol 37

Place	Date	Hour	Summary of Events and Information	Remarks and references to Appendices
Telgam	1/3/19		Visited D.HQ - voted OC 105 Field Ambulance	
	2/3/19		Visited O.HQ	
	3/3/19		Visited D.HQ, attended Cadres Solomi - sent G.O.C. reference Battycolonia. I was arranged to return to Beads at once. Arranged with GOC to ask GSO1 to send Colors for 11th Royal Scots out to France.	
	4/3/19		Visited D.HQ. Arranged to send Lorry to Watton to meet 10th 73rd, who returned to Rest Area from Italy. Sent Order to M 76 9 Bn MacRoberts. Read CO 11th Royal Scots to hand over Colours.	
	5/6/19 6/3		Visited D.HQ daily	
	7/3/19		Read letter of Sympathy also D.HQ	

(signature)

Army Form C. 2118.

WAR DIARY
or
INTELLIGENCE SUMMARY.

(Erase heading not required.)

Instructions regarding War Diaries and Intelligence Summaries are contained in F. S. Regs., Part II. and the Staff Manual respectively. Title pages will be prepared in manuscript.

Place	Date	Hour	Summary of Events and Information	Remarks and references to Appendices
Julgur	11/9	—	Battalion reported for training from OC of 104th Troops	W
	14/9	—	Inspection of Lines developed	W
	15/9	—	Visited D.R.O.; looked at O.R.O. scheme of march for Batt. Looked at training areas & Co's to be returned to. Bn. to S.C.S.I. School.	W
	16/9	—	Visited Adm. General Developing ordered; looked at M.T.; O.R.N. Workshops, also OC Trans & fixed up the examination committee	W
	17/9	—	Visited D.O.R.O.; looked in O.R.O. instructions to units thence on to school to view Cadre review rally. Visited Adm. of Corps C/S Staff to fit & who asked for motor f. Salunga School to take over the Produce law Agr. & Ag. & Bn. reference early inspection	W

(10540) Wt.W4900/P713. 750,000. 2/18. E & S.S.S. Forms/C./2118/11.
D. D. & L., London, E.C.

WAR DIARY
or
INTELLIGENCE SUMMARY.

(Erase heading not required.)

Army Form C. 2118.

Place	Date	Hour	Summary of Events and Information	Remarks and references to Appendices
Shipra	18/4		Visited DADOS 3rd Divn: pictures unchecked & arranged to — S.O.R. visited D.H.Q. who arranged to move Batts. AB,G,y,y not yet to hand for several hours (Gunners were)	W
	19/4		Visited Div. H.Q., also DADoS 30th Divn of R.A unchecked. 21,23°+23° Div: Artilly + Fys) dates for R.A unchecked Other gunner unchecked.	W
	20/4		Visited D.H.Q., visited I.O.M & C. Makayyer & Gunner refusers — instructions	W
	21/4		Inspected W. Store, Ichilds & Battys. 69 R.F.A. Bde also 13.Col. 35 Div. Train with G.O.C & Staff.	W
	22/4		Inspected W. Stores Hyped Govt Fre H.Q. & Railhead & Bde. R.F.A. 30th Div: about Bathed 149 Fde R.F.A. 30 Divn also N.Q. Div Arty. 30th Divn.	W

Army Form C. 2118.

WAR DIARY
or
INTELLIGENCE SUMMARY.
(Erase heading not required.)

Instructions regarding War Diaries and Intelligence Summaries are contained in F.S. Regs., Part II. and the Staff Manual respectively. Title pages will be prepared in manuscript.

Place	Date	Hour	Summary of Events and Information	Remarks and references to Appendices
Selypus	23/9		Inspected three 3rd B. C.F. Tanks & 9th K.H.us.	Y
	24/9		Noted till noon. I am Almer. Indus G60 St Omer. referred & Leave for R.V.O. Indus DADOS 3rd Driv reference stores of 10 & Corps Cmd now at Cop of 4 Th Royal Scots	Y
	23/9		Noted. Inspected three regiments SA of 17th Bde. above HQ CRD Bullecourt 63 RSA Bde. Inspected out 7 & RE elever No. 6 Div trans. + 10 Dunkirk.	Y
	26/9		Took D. HQ & DADOS 9 Corps reference labour for 35 & 86.7 all. attacked men are being used. above by Aske of DAG GHQ whose notes the work of carry as an IEO. No visible work appears 15 to 20 tons short. equipment. Nilchose among as daily.	W

Army Form C. 2118.

WAR DIARY
or
INTELLIGENCE SUMMARY.
(Erase heading not required.)

Instructions regarding War Diaries and Intelligence Summaries are contained in F. S. Regs., Part II. and the Staff Manual respectively. Title pages will be prepared in manuscript.

Place	Date	Hour	Summary of Events and Information	Remarks and references to Appendices
Belgium	27/4	—	Inspected HQ 106 Infty Bde also 12th HLI 16th HLI 17th Royal Scots, HQ 35 DAC also No 1, 2 +3 Sec DAC.	U
	28/4	—	Conversation with C O of Neighbour & Bgd South RFA 696 Nox C Brown reymen. New Grp. References sent to over of 35th Bgd attached to me for duty to report to 06 200 X G Bas Buffs. CRA 35 Div cables references to reference in RA Works of 35 Divn.	U
	3/4		Inspected 50 now Ag 106Bde. Q Stans 16 Sqn NSLD 104 FR B Pers to Cadres leaving for England.	U

Col Shorn
Major
CRA o[f]
35th Divn

www.ingramcontent.com/pod-product-compliance
Lightning Source LLC
Chambersburg PA
CBHW081525160426
43191CB00011B/1687